ANALYZING
ISSUES

Science
Technology
& Society

Canadian Cataloguing in Publication Data
Main entry under title:

Analyzing issues: science, technology, & society

Includes bibliographical references.

ISBN 1-895579-33-3

1. Technology - Social aspects. 2. Critical thinking.
I. Galbraith, Donald I., 1936

T14.5.A54 1996   303.48'3 C96-932261-5

Consulting Editor: Jonathan Bocknek
Production Coordination: Francine Geraci
Cover Design: Kerry Designs
Text Design: Heidy Lawrance Associates

Trifolium Books Inc.
a Fitzhenry & Whiteside Company
195 Allstate Parkway,
Markham, Ontario L3R 4T8

In the United States:
Fitzhenry & Whiteside Limited
121 Harvard Avenue, Suite 2
Allston, Massachusetts 02134

www.fitzhenry.ca   godwit@fitzhenry.ca

Fizthenry & Whiteside acknowledges with thanks the Canada Council for the Arts, the Government of Canada through its Book Publishing Industry Development Program, and the Ontario Arts Council for their support in our publishing program.

Printed and bound in Canada
10 9 8 7 6 5 4 3 2 1

ACKNOWLEDGMENTS

"One person can make a *difference*." This statement, as true for issues as it is for so many other situations, has been worn so well that it runs the risk of lapsing into cliché. And yet, this book would never have seen the light of day were it not for Trudy Rising of Trifolium Books. She embraced the kernel of an idea, planted it gently in a mix of opinions from across the country, then gave it time to take root, break ground, and seek the Sun.

This book's publication would not have been possible without the commitment and support of a great many other people, as well. We thank our students from whom our ideas emanated over the years. The thoughtful and thorough editing provided by our editor, Jonathan Bocknek, was essential for the book's development and for it, we sincerely thank him. We would also like to thank the early reviewers of our first draft who provided us with ideas for additions, deletions, and changes for the better: Kyn Barker, Lynda Bolzon, Barry LeDrew, James Leuwko, Dr. Brian McAndrews, Janice Palmer, and Henry Pasma. Small as this book is, we have spent three and one-half years developing it. Just what is important to include? How much is too much? We hope that we have met your needs.

Only we, of course, are responsible for the final inclusions. If you find any matters that require correction or amplification, we hope you will notify us through our publisher. As well, if you have additional ideas you think we should provide to help other students become adept at issues analysis, we hope you will not hesitate to contact our publisher, Trifolium Books Inc.

The Authors

FEATURES OF THIS BOOK

This book has been developed with two related, but differently focused goals in mind: (1) to provide opportunities for practicing critical thinking skills related to issues analysis, and (2) to apply those skills directly in the seeking of resolutions to issues. Some of the features we've included in order to address these two outcomes are as follows:

QUOTATIONS   Starting each chapter, and sprinkled throughout the book, representative viewpoints from scientists, technologists, educators, and authors are provided to stimulate thought, focus discussion, and synthesize key ideas related to analyzing issues about science, technology, and society.

EXERCISES   Practical, thought-provoking questions have been developed to exercise the mind, as well as to put into practice the skills and ideas outlined in the main text. We urge you to do as many of these as you can. By providing a number of different techniques, our purpose is to give you the opportunity to discover which ones work most effectively for you.

SIDE-BARS   Throughout, you will find special sections that are boxed off from the text and Exercises. These are more than "interest boxes." They provide practical suggestions, examples, related ideas to think about, and connections to the world beyond the classroom.

ARTICLES   The numerous newspaper and magazine articles reproduced in this book are spotlighted through the Exercises. Some articles provide familiar backdrops for practicing and developing thinking skills. Others are more useful in providing full-scale application and synthesis of those skills. The articles were carefully selected to provide flexibility in their use; they may be used and reused for different ways of analyzing their content.

GROUP STRATEGIES   Although any of the strategies for analyzing issues can be done independently, with a large group, or even at a distance using computer- or video-conferencing, we have written all the Exercises to be done in small groups. As this book will show, most societal issues are explored not by individuals, but by groups of individuals, often with very different goals. Thus, developing effective group skills is not only practical, but also essential. You may have done a great deal of group (cooperative) work before; if so, we suggest you help others "gear up," since it takes a while to do it well. A group of about four is the ideal size. An advantage of the team approach is the increased information that becomes available for use. When ideas and experiences are combined, a statement from one person can trigger new ideas in another. In structured groups everyone, whether assertive or diffident, is obliged to contribute. The group benefits when everyone's ideas can be encouraged and harnessed to the group's goals.

CONTENTS

PROLOGUE: WHAT THIS BOOK IS ABOUT 1

CHAPTER 1 WHAT IS A SCIENCE AND TECHNOLOGY ISSUE? 3
    Sidebar: The Unpredictable Laser 5
    Exercise 5
The Language of Issues 7
Viewpoints 8
    Exercise 9
    Article: Danube Diverted for Hydro Project 9
    Article: Keeping Deer in Check 10
    Exercise 12
    Article: Why Diamonds Are Not an Esker's Best Friend ... 12
    Issues in Science, Technology, and Society 13
    Exercise 13

CHAPTER 2 STRATEGIES FOR WORKING IN A GROUP 15
    Sidebar: Choosing Your Group 16
Brainstorming 16
Concept Mapping 17
    Exercise 19
    Article: Seeking Redress 20
Think-Pair-Share 21
Roundtable 21
    Exercise 21
Jigsaw 22
    Exercise 23
Academic Controversy 24
    Exercise 26
    Article: Private or Public–Who Should Control Our Water Supply? .. 27
The "Best" Way to the "Right" Answer 28

CHAPTER 3 **FOCUSING YOUR THINKING** **29**

Article: Clean up Great Lakes, Watchdog Demands **30**

Research **31**

Exercise **33**

Article: Big Mackerel Attack **35**

Article: Fishermen Fear They'll Be the Fall Guys **36**

Sidebar: Risk/Benefit Analysis **38**

Exercise **38**

Article: Saskatchewan Dam Wars Prove Nature Always Loses **41**

Article: Gypsy Moth Outbreak May Lead to Quarantine **43**

CHAPTER 4 **PRESENTATIONS** **45**

Debates **46**

Sidebar: Keep to the Issue! **48**

Exercise **49**

Article: Genetic Testing Boom Raises Ethical Questions **50**

Role Playing **52**

Sidebar: Commissions and Task Forces **52**

Exercise **53**

Sidebar: Suggestions for Role Playing a Hearing About
Public Water Supplies **54**

Dramatic Presentations **55**

Sidebar: The Fiction in Science Fiction **56**

Exercise **57**

Article: Caffeine Addiction Not a Myth **58**

EPILOGUE **59**

Appendix: Alternative Role Play–The Acid Rain Debate **61**

Setting the Scene **61**

Sidebar: Guiding the Commission **63**

Character Roles **64**

References **72**

Credits **74**

PROLOGUE: WHAT THIS BOOK IS ABOUT

People often have automatic "knee-jerk reactions" to complex problems: crime– "lock them up!" AIDS–"serves them right!" landfill– not in my back- yard!" guns–"ban them!" bicy- clists–"pests!" Knee-jerk reactions are not the exclusive preserve of liberals or conservatives, of bosses or workers, of young or old, of men or women. Everyone has them. Everyone makes them.

Just as reflex reactions in the body bypass the brain, knee-jerk reactions are often formed without the benefit of the higher-order thinking of which almost everyone is capable. Even so, whether they come from the gut, the heart, or the head, knee-jerk reactions are honest responses to questions that challenge our beliefs, our fears, and our desires. They can be a valu- able starting point for exploring the maze of viewpoints that characterize issues. But stating an opinion too quickly means that you may not have considered impor- tant questions such as:

- What are the facts?

- What solutions have other people considered?

- What are the short-term and long-term consequences?

- How will these solutions affect me, my family, others in my community and the world, other living things?

- How will these solutions affect future generations?

This book provides both general ideas and concrete strategies for analyzing issues in society–problems that invariably involve aspects of science and technology. For these science-technology-society (STS) issues, there are practical skills for generating and evaluating ideas, interpreting arguments, and presenting all sides of a question to an audience. You will gain insight and experience in how you form opinions and how a group goes about deciding on a course of action.

Sample articles about issues new, old, and ongoing are included to stimulate thought and discussion. There are also questions based on these articles, which you can do with little or no further research. And you could apply the same questions, with only minimal adaptation, to whatever issue is currently in the news.

Because people have different experiences, different concerns, different ideas of right and wrong, many issues can never be resolved to everyone's satisfaction. Meanwhile, new problems arise with every advance in science and technology. In spite of this, we do deal with issues, and we do chart the course of society by our collective decisions: locally, nationally, and internationally. It is our hope that this book will help you, now and for the rest of your life, to make a valuable contribution to this process.

"The open society, the unrestricted access to knowledge, the unplanned and uninhibited association of [people] for its furtherance–these are what may make a vast, complex, ever growing, ever changing, ever more specialized and expert technological world, nevertheless a world of human community."

J. Robert Oppenheimer, *Science and the Common Understanding*

WHAT IS A SCIENCE AND TECHNOLOGY ISSUE? 1

"Science and technology are essential social enterprises, but alone they can only indicate what can happen, not what should happen. [What should happen] involves human decisions about the use of knowledge."
National Science Education Standards

Nearly everyone today accepts that dissection of human corpses is a necessary part of a medical education. Many people donate their bodies to medical schools for this purpose. But in the not-too-distant past, human dissection was a divisive issue. Many people believed that dissection constituted a sacrilegious invasion of the human person, while others held that medical students needed the hands-on experience and understanding that only dissection could provide.

By the early 1700s, this issue had been largely resolved, and our scientific understanding of the human body progressed dramatically. Modern technological innovations such as artificial limbs and organ transplants would not be possible without this understanding. But related questions about dissection still linger. Should junior and senior high school students across the country dissect frogs when frog populations are dwindling? Is it acceptable to dissect animals such as worms, but not cats or dogs or primates? Do "virtual dissections" on computer represent a viable alternative?

Questions such as these invite a spectrum of responses. They are issues—matters about which people have differing ideas and opinions. People have different ideas and opinions about many things. For example, there are different opinions about what the words "science" and "technology" mean. But most people probably wouldn't consider the definitions of these words to be an issue.

So what **is** an issue? For that matter, what are science, technology, and society? The diagram below presents one way to think about the meanings of these words.

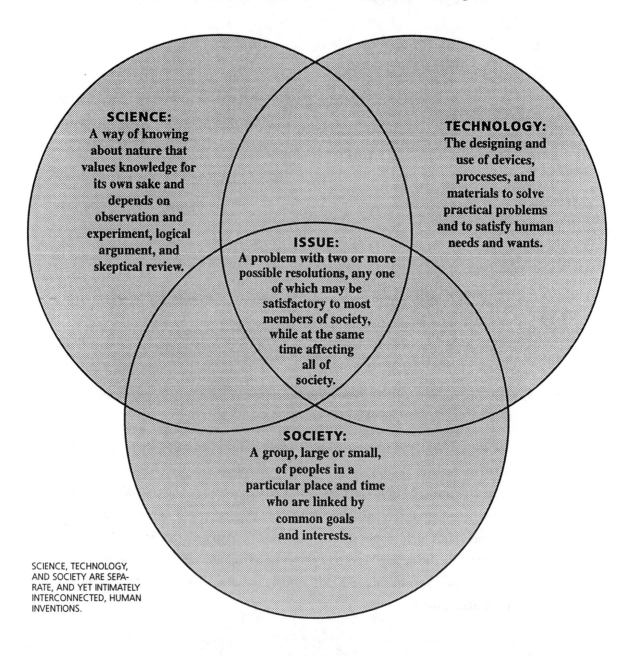

SCIENCE:
A way of knowing about nature that values knowledge for its own sake and depends on observation and experiment, logical argument, and skeptical review.

TECHNOLOGY:
The designing and use of devices, processes, and materials to solve practical problems and to satisfy human needs and wants.

ISSUE:
A problem with two or more possible resolutions, any one of which may be satisfactory to most members of society, while at the same time affecting all of society.

SOCIETY:
A group, large or small, of peoples in a particular place and time who are linked by common goals and interests.

SCIENCE, TECHNOLOGY, AND SOCIETY ARE SEPARATE, AND YET INTIMATELY INTERCONNECTED, HUMAN INVENTIONS.

If, perhaps, you "take issue" with any of them, try to arrive at a consensus. (A consensus is an agreement that satisfies most, but usually not all, of the people involved in making a decision.) In this chapter you will analyze differences between science and technology, and you will consider the range of viewpoints there may be about a specific issue.

THE UNPREDICTABLE LASER

Lasers have a multitude of uses today. For example, the bar codes printed on price tags, books, and grocery items are read with lasers. Surgeons operate using them. Compact discs are "read" by them.

But when lasers were invented as scientific research tools in the early 1960s, scientists could find no practical applications for them beyond the laboratory!

In today's economic climate, taxpaying members of society appear to have little sympathy for under-funded scientists working on seemingly frivolous research subjects. As a result, government funding of science is frequently restricted to research projects that are assumed to have practical, marketable applications. And yet this episode from history illustrates the difficulty of accurately predicting the outcomes of scientific research. As you can see, the funding for so-called "pure research," that is, research for which there is no perceived practical value, is itself an issue. An important one? Each society, as a whole, decides.

Exercise

All the following questions are intended for discussion within a group.

1. (a) Before meeting with your group, rank each of the issues listed below on a scale of 1 to 5, where 1 indicates you think the issue is of minor importance and 5 indicates it is of major importance. Then compare your rankings with the rest of the group. Where groups members have ranked differently, encourage each person to explain their reasons.
   - air pollution
   - world population growth
   - use of nuclear energy
   - spread of AIDS
   - the need for clean water

continued ▶

- public access to information
- toxic chemicals in the environment
- extinction of plant species
- extinction of animal species
- noise pollution

(b) For each of the issues listed in part (a), discuss how science is related to it.

(c) For each of the issues listed in (a), discuss how technology is related to it.

2. Describe how each of the following technological developments has affected society.

(a) the telephone
(b) modern medicines
(c) skyscrapers
(d) reduced-fat foods
(e) the Internet

3. For each of the technologies in question 2, describe the science that was needed for it to be developed. (Be as specific as possible.)

4. The following statements and questions are related to science, technology, and/or society. Analyze each statement, discussing how it relates to one, two, or all three of these.

(a) Why don't frogs freeze to death in winter?
(b) How should braces be fastened to move the teeth as easily as possible?
(c) The dump should be far away from the city limits.
(d) We'll never send people to Mars.
(e) Cars need oil in their engines.
(f) A new element has been discovered recently.
(g) Illegal drugs have a lasting effect on our ability to function effectively.
(h) Certain strains of bacteria are becoming resistant to antibiotics.
(i) A set of Siamese twins was successfully separated at a Toronto hospital.
(j) Why can't children drive cars?
(k) How does that stomach medicine work?
(l) It is possible to determine the sex of a child before birth.

5. Which of the items in question 4 do you consider to be issues? Keeping to the question of whether or not each is an issue (while avoiding the question of what should be done about it), try to reach a consensus within the group.

THE LANGUAGE OF ISSUES

Analyzing issues involves paying close attention to the words that people use. For example, consider the word "safe" in the question, "Is the drug safe?" If one million people take it without side effects, is it safe? If one of those people develops headaches, is it still safe? If ten of them develop high blood pressure, is it still safe? If people are assuming different meanings for the same word, they may be debating with someone about different things!

There were some words similar to "safe" in the Exercise earlier. Think about the words "effectively" and "successfully" in question 4. How clear is their meaning? Another word that causes misunderstanding is "environmentalist." It is sometimes used as an epithet, akin to "tree-hugger." But why can't someone who makes a living from the environment, such as a farmer or a logger, be an environmentalist? Can you live in an urban area and be an environmentalist?

Two other words that are common to discussions about issues are "fact" and "opinion." Often, these words are set up as opposites, where facts are assumed to be unconditionally true and objective, while opinions are disfavored because they are subjective. But opinions can be valuable, and facts can be inaccurate or misleading. For example, in response to the question, "Is the drug safe?," a pharmaceutical company's answer may differ from that of a regulating agency. A physician's answer may differ from a naturopath's. You always need to think about the source of facts and opinions, and assess to what degree you trust, or can be persuaded to trust, that source.

Whenever you discuss issues, you make decisions–silently, in your mind–about which facts are worth mentioning, and which ideas are worth considering. What you decide to exclude may be as revealing of your opinions as what you bring to the discussion.

> *"Attention to the language of the discourse is important. Much clarification can be gained by focusing on the language as an expression of values and priorities. Whenever someone talks to you about benefits and costs of a particular project, don't ask 'What benefits?' ask 'Whose benefits and whose costs?'"*
>
> Dr. Ursula Franklin, *The Real World of Technology*

VIEWPOINTS

Opinions, knee-jerk or otherwise, are influenced by a host of factors including age, sex, life experience, work experience, knowledge, education, social status, beliefs, and values. When people state their views about an issue, they are giving voice to lthis "background maze" of factors. And it's often possible to detect one, several, or many viewpoints that they are consciously or unconsciously expressing. For example:

- ecological–concern for the health and welfare of the natural environment
- economic–concern for profitability
- scientific–concern for knowledge for its own sake
- egocentric–concern for personal needs and wants
- moral/ethical–concern for "rightness" and "wrongness"
- technological–concern for the best solution under the circumstances
- aesthetic–concern for beauty
- emotional–concern for feelings and emotions
- historical–concern for learning from past experiences

You could probably think of many other examples of viewpoints. The more you t hink about them and look for them, the easier it is to notice them. For instance, a news report that refers to "harvesting trees" and "managing wilderness" creates a very different impression from a report that mentions "devastating clear-cuts" and "destruction."

Viewpoints, however, don't exist in isolation, nor are they mutually exclusive. For example, if you are thinking about the cost of college or university tuition fees, you might express a student's viewpoint: "Keep fees low!" But as a member of a tax-paying family, you might also feel, "Why should the government subsidize students?" From a historical viewpoint, you might think, "Education is essential to a society, and nobody should be hindered by lack of money." But looking at the economy, you might believe that "Government's first priority should be to get rid of the deficit."

Because issues, and especially STS issues, can be so complex, it's tempting to simplify them by substituting viewpoints for the people who hold them. However, this has the effect of reducing people to stereotypes. So, for example, if people are referred to as "pro-choice" or "anti-logging," they can be quickly agreed with or dis-missed on the basis of their label, rather than on the substance of their arguments. People are more than the sum total of their viewpoints. And so are issues.

STS Exercise

All the questions below are for group discussion.
Read the article "Danube Diverted for Hydro project."

(a) What are the complaints from Hungary, and what viewpoints are expressed in those complaints?

(b) What is the ecological view?

(c) Which of the viewpoints are in favor of the hydroelectric project?

Danube Diverted for Hydro Project
Slovakia goes ahead despite Hungarian protest

Prague (AP)–Traffic on the Danube River was diverted into a 32-kilometre channel on Slovak territory Tuesday, as part of a controversial new hydroelectric project that has poisoned relations between Slovakia and Hungary.

Hungary has complained to the World Court, saying the Gabeikovo dam project could cut water supplies to millions of its citizens and alter the border with the Slovak lands. Ecologists said it could dry out unique wetlands harboring animal species and birds threatened with extinction.

On Oct. 20, international navigation of the Danube was interrupted southeast of the Slovak capital, Bratislava, to allow the river to be diverted.

Czechoslovakia's CSTK news agency quoted manager Karon And saying four Slovak ships tested the canal Monday and it was opened for traffic Tuesday.

He said it would take 10 more days before 174 ships, backed up since the original channel was closed, could pass through. They have been waiting at Komarno, west of the dam.

The project diverts the Danube, which forms part of the boundary between Slovakia and Hungary, into a clear channel deeper inside Slovakia.

The Danube starts in Germany and empties into the Black Sea.

Slovak authorities, badly in need of industrial projects as they split from the more-industrialized Czechs, said the project does not change the border, and the construction is irreversible.

The separation of Czechoslovakia into independent Czech and Slovak republics [was] planned for Jan. 1 [1993].

Czechoslovakia and Hungary signed a treaty to build the dam in 1977.

Hungary never built its part of the project and abrogated the treaty in 1990.

(Reprinted with permission from Associated Press)

Exercise

Read the article "Keeping Deer in Check."

(a) How do the viewpoints of the landowners differ from the viewpoints of the hunters?

(b) What other viewpoints are mentioned in the article?

(c) Identify any other viewpoints you think are missing.

(d) What is the issue here?

Keeping Deer in Check

Population boom poses dilemma

by Bruce Masterman

RED DEER LAKE–Ron Chase was a hunter until he moved out of Calgary to a foothills ranch 19 years ago.

But when a hunter shot a huge whitetail buck that lived on his land, Chase was so upset he hung up his guns forever.

"I could never shoot a deer now," Chase, 58, said in an interview.

"I feel like I'm their host."

A few miles to the northeast, fellow rancher Dave Cannon recounts how the area's deer population has exploded in the past several years, taking a heavy toll on his crops and hay stacks.

Cannon, 72, is one of the few landowners in the area who welcome hunters.

"We like to see them get a few deer and thin out the population," he said.

The divergent stances of Chase and Cannon reflect the dilemma facing provincial wildlife managers trying to manage the burgeoning whitetail and mule deer population in a 968-square-mile area around Calgary.

The region has been designated a "bow zone" since 1974 when the province began restricting big game hunters to using archery equipment.

The move to eliminate high-powered rifles was prompted by growing safety concerns fuelled by increased development of small farms and residential acreages.

Over the years, however, deer have flourished. Bow hunters complain many landowners won't give them access to hunt while landowners counter they either don't want the deer harmed or they don't like strangers showing up at their door to seek permission.

Squeezed by diminishing habitat gobbled up by development, the deer have been raiding crops and vegetable gardens. Many are hit by cars.

Ron Bjorge, Alberta Fish and Wildlife's regional wildlife biolo-gist, said there are too many deer. The animals face death by starvation or disease if they continue to increase and if a harsh winter occurs, he said.

"There's a limit to the number of deer the land will hold and the community will tolerate," Bjorge said. "We're at that limit now."

The province is studying ways to increase hunters' fall harvest of deer. Some options being considered include extending the hunting season or allowing other methods such as shotguns, blackpowder rifles or even crossbows.

The government last year allowed hunters in the bow zone to shoot two antlerless deer–does or young bucks–in addition to one mature mule and whitetail buck.

Bjorge said he's still waiting for results of 1990 hunter success surveys before recommending any regulation changes to Edmonton. No changes are planned for this fall.

The government estimates the

bow zone contains 1,400 whitetail and 1,550 mule deer. In 1989, 834 mule deer hunters killed 102 deer while 836 whitetail hunters took 86 animals.

Bjorge said the total harvest is about one third of the ideal target number.

While deer numbers are high throughout the bow zone, Bjorge noted they pose a real problem in the Millarville-Red Deer Lake area, where hunting is tightly limited.

On a two-hour, late-afternoon tour of the area last week, Bjorge counted 120 mule deer, 34 white-tails and one elk.

He said the division may launch an educational program to explain to local landowners the importance of reducing deer through hunting.

"Hunting is the primary tool used in wildlife management to keep populations in line with biological and community expectations," Bjorge said.

"To do that, hunters need access to the land."

Many area residents oppose a longer season–it now lasts from early September to the end of November–or to allow any kind of firearms.

"It's horrible living out here in hunting season," said 14-year resi-dent Sally Gregg.

She said residents are constantly besieged by strangers knocking on their doors at all hours asking for permission to hunt. It's unsettling to have strange vehicles entering residents' remote driveways, said Gregg, adding she isn't opposed to hunting.

She said that while the majority of bowhunters are responsible and don't bother residents, a minority often break the rules and cause problems.

Many residents interviewed by the Herald questioned the effective-ness of bowhunters in reducing deer numbers.

But Springbank-area resident Dave Coupland, Alberta Bow-hunters Association, regulations director, bristles when bowhunters' ability is questioned.

He said archers could effectively thin out deer herds if landowners were more co-operative. While a season extension would help increase the kill, Coupland said his association opposes any move to allow shotguns or muzzle loaders in the bow zone.

Landowners would be even less willing to grant access permission to hunters using anything but con-ventional archery equipment, said Coupland, a 46-year-old Calgary architect.

Even more contentious, however, is a proposal from the Okotoks Fish and Game Association to allow the use of crossbows in the bow zone. Crossbows now are illegal for hunt-ing but it's not against the law to own one or use it for target shooting.

Ralph Lane, association past-pres-ident who lives on an acreage near Okotoks, said the crossbow is a more lethal weapon than a standard compound recurve or longbow.

Crossbows are silent, can be fit-ted with telescopic sights like rifles and require relatively little skill to use, he said.

But Coupland condemns cross-bows saying legalizing them would encourage their use by poachers and make land-owners even more nervous.

Lane, however, said government statistics show no poachers caught in the last three years used a crossbow.

Meanwhile, Chase and several other landowners said they don't begrudge the deer the crops and gar-den produce they forage. Local resi-dents learn to drive slowly to avoid hitting deer, especially in early morning and evening, Chase said.

But many people have learned the hard way.

Okotoks RCMP report deer last year were involved in 100 traffic accidents resulting in damage of more than $5000. The year before there were 107 accidents.

All the deer were killed. Several human injuries and one death also resulted.

Officer Roger Gluckie, in charge of the High River Fish and Wildlife office, said only six complaints have been received this winter from resi-dents concerned with deer and elk eating hay and ornamental shrubs.

Up to 25 complaints have been received in harsher winters, he said.

Gluckie recommends rural resi-dents discourage deer by fencing hay stacks and placing their pet dogs' houses closer to gardens. He also suggests spreading commer-cially-available blood meat–dried slaughterhouse product–around areas attractive to deer.

Scarecrows and small portable radios also discourage deer, Gluckie said.

Exercise

Read the article, "Why Diamonds Are Not an Esker's Best Friend".

(a) What are the viewpoints presented in the article?

(b) What other viewpoints might there be?

(c) Suggest an organization or institution that might be an appropriate moderator for this issue.

Why Diamonds Are Not an Esker's Best Friend

by Ed Struzik

Will a new northern Canadian diamond mine do damage to the planet? When Australia's Broken Hill Proprietors, the world's fifth-largest mining company, joined forces with a small Kelowna, British Columbia outfit to build a $500 million diamond mine in the Northwest Territories, the question was hardly discussed. Mine boosters continue to argue that diamond extraction involves none of the harmful chemicals associated with other mining. And even Monte Hummel, head of World Wildlife Fund Canada, admits that the risk of limited mining to the local environment is not the issue. But now there's a darker shadow on the whole glittery business: news about the cumulative impact of several mines in the central Arctic on wildlife, such as the Bathurst caribou herd, and on sensitive eskers.

Eskers are narrow ridges of sand and gravel left behind by meltwater rivers that flowed through Ice Age glaciers. Early results of a study initiated last summer suggest that eskers are important to the well-being of a variety of northern animals, including wolves, grizzly bears, Arctic and red foxes, wolverines, rodents, and the birds of prey that feed on them. Fritz Mueller, a Northwest Territories scientist, says about 75 percent of all bear and wolf dens are located on tundra eskers, likely because that is where the best ground is located.

"I suppose every biologist who has worked in the North knows this," he says. "But no one has tried to quantify it." The trouble is, mining companies want to use the sand and gravel from eskers to build service roads in and around their operations and possibly to a seaport on the Arctic Coast. No one knows what the impact of that will be.

Such studies take years to complete, so Mueller and his colleagues will not have the data they need to prove their case before an environmental-assessment review panel gets under way later this year.

"On the one side you're going to have a well-rehearsed, polished submission from the mining companies," says Hummel. "On the other we'll have the scientists with little time to back up their broader concerns."

STS Exercise

All the questions below are for group discussion.

1. What viewpoints might you consider in examining the following issues?

   (a) the withdrawal of a life-support system from someone who is being kept alive only by means of that system

   (b) the damage done to the Earth by the proliferation of humans

2. In the 1960s, satirist Tom Lehrer wrote and performed a song called "Pollution," which included the following lines:

   "See the halibuts and the sturgeons
   Being wiped out by detergeons.
   Fish gotta swim and birds gotta fly.
   But they don't last long if they try.
   Pollution, pollution,
   You can use the latest toothpaste,
   And then rinse your mouth with industrial waste."

   (a) What is the viewpoint expressed here, and how relevant is it today?

   (b) What do you think has changed since the 1960s, both in the actual state of water pollution and in society's perception of the issue?

   (c) Think of current popular songs that express a point of view about an issue. What are the issues that people are concerned with now? What viewpoints are expressed in the songs?

ISSUES IN SCIENCE, TECHNOLOGY, AND SOCIETY

The interaction of science, technology, and society is complex. In the course of discussing issues, you may hear someone say, "The more I get to know, the less I'm sure of." That's because issues spawn at least as many questions as they do answers. Recognizing what lies behind the issues–the science, the technology, the pulse of society, and the historical context–will give you an advantage in forming your own opinions, and considering those of others.

"Collections of people remain individuals until a single event or purpose or emotion molds them into groups, and ... then the group lives, feels, and thinks in a way of its own, superior in energy and intensity to the activity of any one of its members."
Gilbert Highet, *The Art of Teaching*

Working with other people is a fact of life–in courses, in jobs, on committees, or wherever you spend your time. In musical groups and sports teams, individuals have their own ideas and may express them forcefully. But for the good of the group, everyone has to agree finally on the strategy to be followed and on how to implement it. The same is true in society. When dealing with issues, the participation of many people ensures that many different ideas are brought forward and that fair compromises can be made.

There are techniques for working with groups of people, techniques that help them to function effectively. For larger groups, there are the accepted rules of order for meetings, with a chairperson, order of speakers, motions made and seconded, etc. For smaller groups, there are many ways you can organize yourselves, depending on what it is that you want to accomplish.

In this chapter the assumption is you are cooperating in a small group, of about three to six people, to generate ideas about STS issues. (In a later chapter the emphasis will be on analytical thinking; for now the focus is on ideas.) You will aim for wide-ranging ideas (although no research will be necessary), and will attempt to have each individual play a valuable role in the group. In any discussion about issues, there will be disagreements, sometimes very heated disagreements. These make the discussions more interesting, as long as everyone refrains from personal attacks.

The first two techniques below, brainstorming and concept mapping, are informal ways of encouraging all group members to contribute. The techniques that follow are more formal strategies, in which everyone has an assigned role to play.

CHOOSING YOUR GROUP

A group of individuals with abilities in different areas may have more success in co-operative work than a group that is more homogeneous. Some people excel at research, some at logical thinking, some at making models, some at doing exciting or amusing presentations. If you have the option of choosing your colleagues from a larger group, try some random selection method such as drawing cards, pulling straws, or rolling dice. You will probably find you have a mixture of people with different strengths and weaknesses, different personalities, and different viewpoints.

Ideally, you should form new groups periodically. That way you cannot come to depend on one individual who is particularly good at organizing, or coming up with ideas, or doing presentations–you will have the chance to develop all these skills yourself. As well, you will get more experience in working with the dynamics of different groups.

BRAINSTORMING

Brainstorming is frequently a first step in the process of producing workable ideas. In brainstorming, people agree to express to the group whatever ideas about a topic come into their heads. The aim is to inspire each other to generate as many ideas as possible–sensible, off-the-wall, and everything between. One member writes down everything that is suggested, and there is absolutely no discussion about any of the ideas. The cardinal rule of brainstorming is that every suggestion is valid; *no idea is ever ridiculed.* This frees everyone from self-censorship and creates a relaxed, supportive atmosphere for crazy and imaginative notions.

CONCEPT MAPPING

A concept map is a visual representation of the connections between concepts or ideas; it shows ways of organizing them. To start a concept map, you can write the central idea at the top of a large page, then add related ideas and show how they are joined to one another. To make sense of the relationships between the terms, linking words such as "have," "can be," etc. are used. Here are two examples of concept maps. Many variations are possible, though. What is important is how well the map serves the needs of the group (or individual) who is using it.

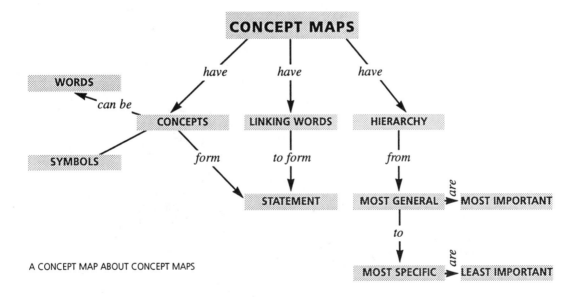

A CONCEPT MAP ABOUT CONCEPT MAPS

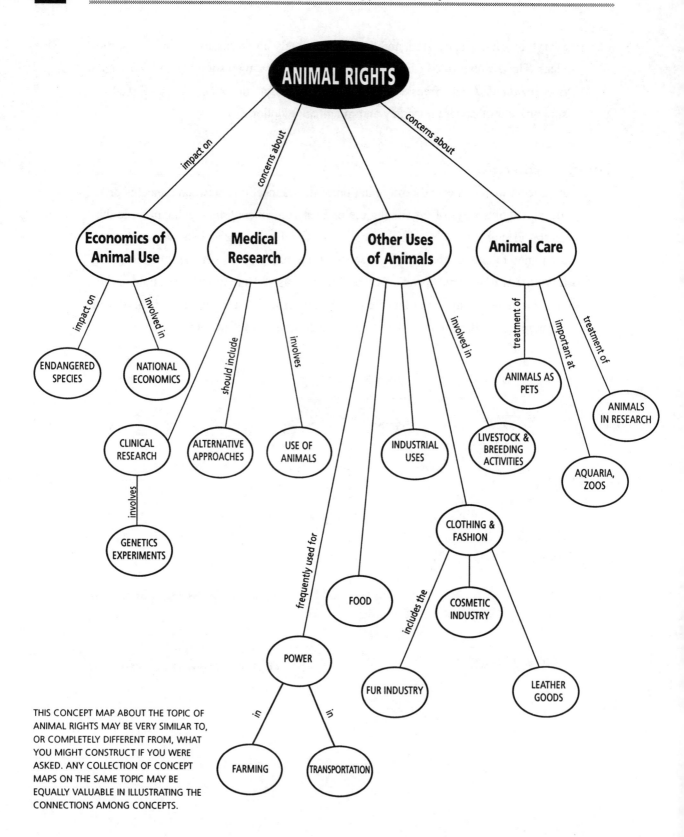

THIS CONCEPT MAP ABOUT THE TOPIC OF ANIMAL RIGHTS MAY BE VERY SIMILAR TO, OR COMPLETELY DIFFERENT FROM, WHAT YOU MIGHT CONSTRUCT IF YOU WERE ASKED. ANY COLLECTION OF CONCEPT MAPS ON THE SAME TOPIC MAY BE EQUALLY VALUABLE IN ILLUSTRATING THE CONNECTIONS AMONG CONCEPTS.

When a group works together on a concept map, everyone can contribute their own ideas, explaining the connections as the map grows. You will find that you begin to see connections that you may not have thought of on your own. The process also gives you insight into how your colleagues' minds are working.

STS Exercise

1. For this question individuals could work on their own maps, then share them with the group. Alternatively, the group could develop a single map that fairly captures the feelings of the members.

    (a) Make a concept map on "logging" using all of the following terms: logging, soil, clearcut harvesting, trees, types, environment, erosion, jobs, machinery, economy, forest products, wildlife, fuel, housing, marketing, pollution, selective harvesting, chemicals, water, waste products.

    (b) Expand the concept map, adding as many more terms as you want or need.

2. Have everyone in the group read the article, "Seeking Redress" (page 20). Agree on a single significant word or concept about the issue that is described in the article, and have the group's recorder write it at the top of a page. Then hold a five-minute brainstorming session to generate at least one page full of diverse, related ideas.

3. On a large sheet of paper, produce a concept map around the word that you chose to use for your brainstorming session. Begin by selecting a word particularly closely related to science or technology. With words and connectors, include as many of the brainstormed ideas as are appropriate in the concept map.

Seeking Redress

Like bulletins from a battlefront, the news about Canada's tainted blood scandal keeps getting worse. Of the more than 1,000 Canadians who contracted AIDs through contaminated transfusions in the 1980s, about 850 accepted compensation in 1994, while 30 others have launched lawsuits against the Red Cross. Two of those cases are scheduled to begin in Toronto this week. But it now appears that at least 12,000 other Canadians received blood containing hepatitis C, a chronic, potentially lethal virus that attacks the liver. Symptoms—which can lie dormant for 10 to 30 years or appear immediately—include debilitating fatigue, impaired mental functioning, hemorrhaging and, finally, liver failure. "All the attention paid to AIDS will pale by the time hepatitis C is in full bloom," predicts Herb Moeller, 49, a Vancouver vice-president of the Hepatitis C Survivors Society.

So far, fewer than 100 of those with hepatitis C have launched individual lawsuits. Many are awaiting the outcome of the ongoing public inquiry into the tainted blood scandal, which they believe will help clear the legal fog that has enveloped the issue of responsibility since it first erupted in the mid-1980s. While they wait, lawyers are drafting class-action suits, a process that allows one plaintiff to argue a case on behalf of all those who may be directly affected by the result. Ottawa lawyer Pierre Lavigne, who is co-counsel on one such suit in Quebec, says that it will be brought against the federal government, Quebec and the Red Cross, because all participated in the decision not to test blood for the presence of the hepatitis C virus. Such tests were adopted by U.S. authorities in 1986, but Canada decided the same year merely to study their effectiveness. Canada began to test for the virus in 1990.

Many hepatitis C victims are particularly angered by that decision, because the AIDS debacle had already alerted officials to the potential impact of contaminated blood. They are also concerned that the slow, if unrelenting, progress of the hepatitis C infection may obscure its tragic impact.

Moeller jokes that he felt lucky to get the "slow one" when he learned he had hepatitis C, not HIV, after multiple transfusions in the early 1980s. But he is dead serious when he talks about the need for establishing a clear trail of responsibility for tainted blood. "Politicians and bureaucrats have lost sight of doing the right thing," he says.

THINK-PAIR-SHARE

In this technique, the group decides on a particular problem to consider, and each person takes the time required to think about their ideas for solutions. Everyone then pairs off with a partner. The partners discuss their ideas together, combining them into a single solution, which is then shared with the group. The whole group together then discusses the solutions of the pairs, modifying them until they can agree on a compromise solution. This exercise is usually done with time limits. One partner from each pair can be the time-keeper, and the other partner can be the one who reports to the group.

ROUNDTABLE

In this problem-solving technique, the group shares one piece of paper and one pen. As you sit around a table, you hand around the paper and pen so that each person can write one line of the solution to the problem. Before you start, you need to agree on guidelines, such as how much time each person is allowed, and whether or not you can "pass" if you want to.

§TS Exercise

1. As a group, select one of the following questions, then use the think-pair-share technique to discuss it. Time limits could be two minutes to think, three minutes as a pair, and five minutes for each pair to share their views.

   (a) Why is it important to eat a balanced diet?

   (b) Why are scientists so concerned about the destruction of tropical rainforests?

   (c) Should we ban all uses of nuclear energy?

   (d) Should smoking be banned from all public places?

continued ▶

2. To try out the roundtable technique, select a problem from question 1 that you have not already discussed.

3. At a recent symposium on the ethical and social implications of medical genetics, a participant presented the following hypothetical circumstance:

> "Suppose that a person were to stand on a bridge over traffic and drop chunks of ice on the passing cars below. Let us further assume that the probability of causing serious damage to a car and its occupants is one chance in four. Given this likelihood that a tragic accident will occur, it can be safely stated that the person will be arrested for misconduct and that society will ask the perpetrator to pay damages.

> "We now ask if comparable conditions pertain to parents, both of whom have been identified as carriers of an allele which could lead to a serious genetic disorder causing babies born with the condition to die with two or three years."

Decide on what technique (or techniques) your group will use to discuss the following questions.

(a) Is the risk of danger to the children born to these parents as great as the risk to drivers passing under the bridge?

(b) If two carrier parents insist on having children, is such an action equivalent to that of the person dropping chunks of ice on passing cars?

(c) Assuming that you support the personal freedom to reproduce, who should pay for the considerable costs of treating the infant with the disease to make its few years of life as painless as possible?

(d) Is there--should there be--an obligation to refrain from knowingly producing offspring who will be a drain on the resources of society?

(e) Is this a good analogy? Can you think of a better one?

JIGSAW

A jigsaw is a more ambitious way of working, in which several groups cooperate. Suppose all the groups are investigating an issue for which considerable research is needed, such as who should do the planning to ensure that the forestry industry can continue to contribute to the country's economy. There are so many questions that could be asked, so many directions that could be taken, so many parts of the country to consider. How can you organize yourselves, without giving too heavy a load of responsibility to any one person?

In a jigsaw, each member of the group is designated to become the expert in one particular area of the topic. If the groups each have four people, you could have experts in (1) types of logging, (2) logging in British Columbia, (3) environmental considerations, and (4) the uses of forest products. The experts from different groups–all the (1)s, all the (2)s, etc. –get together to brainstorm ideas, gather information, and pool what they find. They then go back and share their information with their "home" group.

Jigsaws can be used for virtually any topic. For example, if your group has a long article to read, you could divide it up into parts. Group members could go off into their expert groups to consider their assigned part of the article, then return to the home group to share their findings.

Exercise

The "jigsaw" method of group work is particularly suitable when you need to do a lot of research about a topic. You can, however, try out the jigsaw organization in an exploration of an issue without the need for research about the issue. Three sample issues and how they could be broken down are shown below.

I. The city is trying to decide whether or not to build a new water filtration plant.
    A Effect on municipal taxes
    B Environmental concerns
    C Viewpoints of people living in the area where the plant is to be built
    D Health considerations
II. At the present rate of growth the population of Country X will double in 21 years.
    A Economic considerations
    B Effect on the education system
    C Food factors
    D Health issues

continued ▶

III. A mining company is planning to open a new smelter near a small tourist-dependent community.

    A Environmental considerations

    B Effects of job creation

    C Changes to the way of life of the residents of the community

    D Effect on the profitability of the tourist industry

1. Choose one of the issues to explore.

2. Select home teams of four, as evenly matched as possible.

3. Hold a brief meeting of these home teams to assign a letter--A, B, C, or D--to each individual.

4. Hold meetings of all the A's, all the B's, etc. These are the "expert groups" who now explore their particular aspect of the topic. (Any of the group techniques described earlier in this chapter could be useful in drawing out ideas from all members of the expert groups.)

5. Reassemble the home groups to receive the reports of the experts. In the home group, discuss the issue as a whole, and suggest a course of action.

6. In the larger group, listen to a short report from each home group about (a) their policy statement and (b) how effective they felt the jigsaw technique was in exploring different aspects of the topic.

ACADEMIC CONTROVERSY

If you want to have fun and stretch your mind at the same time, try the technique called academic controversy. In this technique, the group first produces a "position statement" such as:

Clearcutting forests IS/IS NOT the most efficient and cost-effective way of harvesting trees, both now and in the foreseeable future.

You adopt one side of the issue as your own, and argue as forcefully as you can, with all the evidence you can muster, for that side. Then you switch and do the same, with sincere intensity and passion, for the other side. Finally, the entire group comes up with a compromise position statement beginning with "We believe ...," to which everyone must agree. The diagram on page 25 shows how this technique works with a group of four people. Five to seven people could also follow the same steps. If you have eight or more people, you can have an even better academic controversy by forming two separate groups who later merge into two hybrids.

ACADEMIC CONTROVERSY

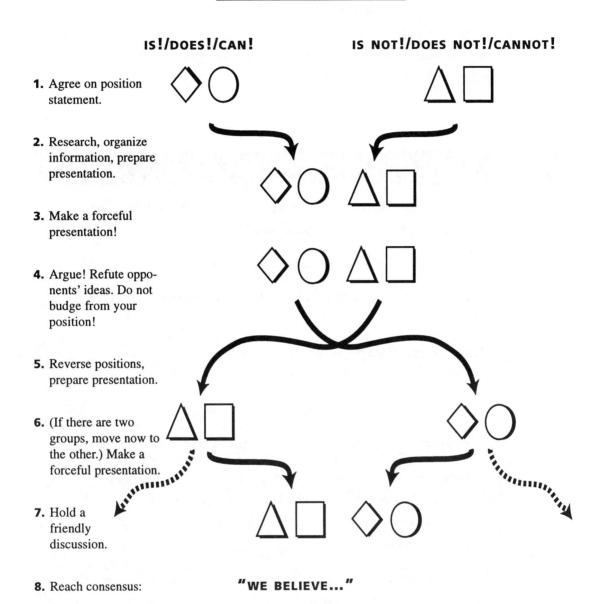

IS!/DOES!/CAN!   **IS NOT!/DOES NOT!/CANNOT!**

1. Agree on position statement.

2. Research, organize information, prepare presentation.

3. Make a forceful presentation!

4. Argue! Refute opponents' ideas. Do not budge from your position!

5. Reverse positions, prepare presentation.

6. (If there are two groups, move now to the other.) Make a forceful presentation.

7. Hold a friendly discussion.

8. Reach consensus: **"WE BELIEVE..."**

THIS SHOWS A GROUP OF FOUR PEOPLE USING THE ACADEMIC CONTROVERSY TECH-
NIQUE, COMING BACK TOGETHER FOR THEIR SECOND PRESENTATIONS AND FINAL STATE-
MENT. IDEALLY, AT STEP 6, RATHER THAN MOVING BACK INTO THE ORIGINAL GROUP, ONE
PAIR SHOULD TRADE PLACES WITH A PAIR FROM A DIFFERENT GROUP, SO THAT EVERYONE
GETS TO HEAR A DIFFERENT SET OF ARGUMENTS.

For an effective academic controversy, the initial position statement is crucial; it needs to be carefully chosen and to be clearly stated so that there can be two and only two sides to the question. You may need considerable time for step 2, depending on how much research is needed. For all the subsequent steps, give yourselves strict time limits, such as 1-5 minutes each.

STS Exercise

All the questions below refer to the article "Private or Public–Who Should Control Our Water Supply?" (pages 27 and 28).

1. Describe the viewpoints that are expressed in the article.

2. Select three or four facts presented in the article. How could you verify them?

3. What kinds of information would you look for in your research, if you were doing an in-depth study of this issue?

4. What contribution can science make to this issue?

5. What contribution can technology make to this issue?

6. Use the article as the basis for carrying out an academic controversy with your group. Adopt the following as the position statement: Municipal water supplies SHOULD/SHOULD NOT be owned and operated by municipal governments.

7. Do a "debriefing" about the effectiveness of the academic controversy exercise in question 6. How well did everyone manage to appear convincing, whether or not they believed their own arguments? What could you improve if you were doing another academic controversy on a different issue?

Private or Public–
Who Should Control
Our Water Supply?

Like many other parts of the world, Ontario's aging waterworks is in need of upgrading. But to do so will cost large amounts of money, money which is difficult to obtain given the tough economic times in which we live.

One possible solution, commonly used in Europe, is to have private interests take over the local public water utilities. Many civic politicians favour this approach but environmentalists are divided over the possible implications. This new solution raises questions as to whether or not private firms would encourage or hinder the cleanup of Ontario's drinking water. Governments simply do not have to the money required to improve the water supply. But if private companies have not taken all of the steps necessary to clean up the water supply, what motivation would they have to do so after they gain control of the system?

Recently, a committee in Halton Region in Ontario voted to begin a request for proposals from private firms to build and run a new $ 435 million water and sewage treatment plant. At this point, no decisions have been made except to say that the regional government is prepared to entertain proposals in order to obtain the best deal for the area.

The problem seems to centre around the fact that treatment plants across the province rely on aging technology, despite years of cleanup legislation pledges. There is also a sense that the drinking water standards are badly out of date.

Typically, water treatment plants use processes aimed at eliminating bacteria from the water using chlorine. But little is done to remove the chemical pollutants which are becoming increasingly common in Lake Ontario. While their levels may fall within government safety standards, many environmentalists are concerned about the cumulative effects of these contaminants. It is estimated that there are some 18 000 new chemicals produced each year and it is vir-

Continued on page 28

Private or Public–
Who Should Control
Our Water Supply?

Continued from page 27

tually impossible to predict what effects any of these might have if they enter our water supply.

The question, however, centres around who will pay for the new technology necessary to maintain and improve the water supply. Historically, the cost of water in Ontario has been very low compared to many regions and this discourages conservation. Even when people in this province are paying for water by the litre, they are really only paying for pumping the water.

And, in the U.K., where the water supply has been privatized and the quality of water arguably improved, the price of water to consumers has risen, on average, since 1989, some 77%.

Checks of the quality of drinking water are usually carried out by municipalities themselves in Ontario. Critics shudder to think of what might happen if there is not a strong regulatory body acting to monitor and protect the water supply. The provincial government focuses on periodically checking the local water treatment plants. Environmentalists are even more concerned about the controls on sewage treat-

ment. Some of the outflow from the sewage plants might become part of the inflow into the water filtration facilities. After household and industrial use, the water, now polluted with everything from garden pesticides to chlorine from water treatment plants, makes its way, via sewers, into the local waterways. The result of all of this is that it places an enormous burden on Lake Ontario. To solve all of these problems will require a great deal of cooperation, money, technology, and input from all of the parties concerned, not the least of which are the consumers.

The "Best" Way to the "Right" Answer

In group work, every person has a role to play. This positive interdependence, where the success of each group member is connected to the success of all the others, goes a long way to develop the team spirit that can make learning exciting. Working in a group, you have probably found that there is no "best" method for examining any problem, just as there is no single "right" answer. But if you approach problems in a number of different ways, there is greater likelihood of more suggestions to consider. Any of the techniques in this chapter will help you to become more aware of the ideas and concerns of your colleagues, as well as your own. Only when as many points as possible have been raised and considered is there likely to be an acceptable resolution of a problem.

*"Like race car drivers who shift in and out of
different gears depending on where they are on the
course, creative people are able to shift in and out of
different types of thinking depending on the needs
of the situation at hand. Sometimes they're open
and probing, and at others they're playful and
off-the-wall. At still other times, they're
critical and faultfinding. And finally,
they're doggedly persistent in
striving to reach their goals."*

Roger von Oech, *Kick in the Seat of the Pants*

Wild and wonderful ideas about issues can be generated by the techniques described
in the previous chapter. But at some point you need to find out more about the
issue, by doing research. Research can help you determine such things as:

• how the issue grew from its historical background and social context;

• what is known about the underlying science and technology;

Clean up Great Lakes, Watchdog Demands

Chlorine cited in new report as key pollutant

BY BRIAN MCANDREW
ENVIRONMENT REPORTER

A Great Lakes watchdog agency is hanging tough in its demands that Canada and the United States rid the world's largest body of fresh water of the worst toxic chemicals.

The International Joint Commission repeated its demand for a greater effort at toxic pollution cleanup in a report released today in Ottawa and Washington.

The report calls on the governments to pay especially close attention to ending the industrial use of chlorine.

The commission, a bilateral agency established by the two countries to monitor Great Lakes water issues, maintained its stand despite massive pressure from the chlorine manufacturing and chlorine-using industries.

More than 300 industry representatives were among the record-setting 1,700 people attending the commission's biannual meeting last fall in Windsor.

The commission's report calls on the two countries to develop a common strategy within two years to stop the dumping of "persistent toxic substances" in the Great Lakes.

Eight of the 11 most persistent toxic substances–chemicals that remain for lengthy periods in the water–contain chlorine or chlorinated compounds including dioxins, PCBs (polychlorinated biphenyls), DDT and hexachlorobenzene.

The chemicals have been linked with health problems

- how other people–scientists, technologists, workers, teachers, politicians, industry leaders, etc.–view the issue;
- what experimental evidence there is to support these views;
- what anecdotal evidence there is to support these views;
- whether any discussions, resolutions, or decisions have been made already.

Once you are armed with this array of information, you are in a position to focus your thinking. Working individually or as part of a group, you begin to develop your own informed opinion on the issue and to consider possible courses of action. After analyzing the risks and benefits of these, your group may be ready to recommend a particular course of action.

in fish, wildlife and humans including cancer, reproductive troubles, declining learning performance and increasing behavioral problems among children, the report says.

"Surely there can be no more compelling self-interest to force us to come to grips with this problem than the spectre of damaging the integrity of our own species and its entire environment," the report says.

A coalition of environmental groups will send a letter today to the federal Environment Minister urging the government to adopt the commission's recommendations.

The letter says there was an "urgent need for your government to develop a national strategy for sunsetting persistent toxic substances such as the use of chlorine and chlorine-based compounds to industrial processes."

It adds: "To date, Canada has failed to develop an adequate regulatory response to the public health and ecological danger presented by persistent toxic substances.

The seven groups signing the letter were Greenpeace, Pollution Probe, Great Lakes United, Canadian Environment Law Association, Sierra Club, Canadian Institute for Environmental Law and Policy and Quebec's Society to Vanquish Pollution.

Environment Canada, shortly before the federal election, took a stand against the commission's proposals.

RESEARCH

How to do research is beyond the scope of this book, but a few guidelines may help you to find material without wasting huge amounts of time. Suppose, for example, you will be doing a project related to the Great Lakes, starting off from the article reproduced here, "Clean up Great Lakes, Watchdog Demands." What are the issues, and which issue will you focus on?

First of all, think of research in two stages: general and specific. At the beginning, you need to find out what sort of references are available. In a library you could look up "Great Lakes" or "International Joint Commission" in a subject index, note a few call numbers, and browse the shelves near those numbers. CD-ROMs are invaluable for references to recent magazine articles that may be relevant. At this point, doing some background reading is beneficial. You can make a note of what types of data are available as graphs and tables, and where to find them. This will help not only in narrowing your focus, but in the later stages of research.

Browsing the World Wide Web can also reveal a wealth of general information. The authors of this book, using a common search engine and the keywords "international joint commission great lakes," found the home page of the International Joint Commission at the top of list. One click brought up the page entitled, *"The International Joint Commission: What It Is, How It Works"* (http://www.great-lakes.net:2200/partners/IJC/html/whatis.html); for background reading, that's a winner! Different search engines work differently, so if you are not successful with one, try another. Or try varying the order or number of your keywords.

Once you, or you and your group, have done some preliminary scanning, and have decided on the focus of your work, you will be looking for more specific information such as facts and figures related to the issue. You may find gold in a library at this stage: atlases, reference works, overviews backed up with data. For example, libraries may have *The Great Lakes: An Environmental Atlas and Resource Book*, published jointly by The Government of Canada and the United States Environmental Protection Agency.

But no library has everything. What can you do if your local library cannot help you? Again, the Internet is invaluable. More and more, government departments are putting all their latest reports on the Web. Since we knew of the existence of the environmental atlas mentioned above, we used a search engine on the World Wide Web, using as keywords "environment canada great lakes environmental atlas." The first search engine found the document itself, as third on the list. The entire atlas is on the Web! All the text, all the photos and maps and tables are there (http://www.cciw.ca/glimr/data/great-lakes-atlas/intro.html). The graphics may be small onscreen, but you could download them for viewing with appropriate software.

Some home pages have their own means of searching. The British Columbia Ministry of the Environment home page, for example, allows searches. You can look for specific publications and read or download whatever you need. In many places, you can send e-mail queries or comments from the home page directly to the individuals involved.

A profusion of information is available from a multitude of sources. The challenge is to decide what is important and what is not, what is reliable and what is suspect, who to believe and who to ignore. Putting your research together and predicting the outcomes of different courses of action require very high-level thinking. Ultimately, such factors as your values, your experiences, your background knowledge, and the way your mind operates will influence your interpretations and the opinions you develop as a result.

STS Exercise

There is a popular saying, "Numbers don't lie." Does this necessarily mean that numbers tell the truth? It is worth considering what truths numbers can tell, and what insights they can give you into an STS issue. For questions 1 to 7 on page 34, use the data in Table 1 as the basis for a group discussion.

TABLE 1 THE GREAT LAKES

	Superior		Michigan		Huron		Erie		Ontario	
	Can	U.S.A	Can	U.S.A	Can	U.S.A	Can	U.S.A	Can	U.S.A
Population living on or near the lake (in millions)[1]	0.2	0.4	n/a	10.1	1.2	1.5	1.7	10.0	5.4	2.7
Shoreline use (as % of total use) — Agricultural	–	–	n/a	20	4	15	21	14	30	33
Residential	–	–	n/a	39	34	42	39	45	25	40
Recreational	–	–	n/a	24	8	4	8	13	15	12
Commercial	–	–	n/a	12	35	32	10	12	18	8
Other	–	–	n/a	5	19	7	22	16	12	7
Water volume (km^3)	12 100		4920		3540		484		1640	
Retention/ Replacement time (in years)	191		99		22		2.6		6	

1. Population Figures for Canada are 1991, for U.S.A. are 1990.
2. Data for shoreline use for Lake Superior are not available.

1. How do you think the data in this table were determined?

2. How reliable are these data? What criteria are you using to decide on reliability?

3. What do you think "on or near the lake" means? What other interpretations could there be?

4. Identify any other data or details that are open to interpretation.

5. Translate this table into a brief, descriptive paragraph, being as clear as possible about what the table "tells you."

6. Re-read the article "Clean up Great Lakes, Watchdog Demands before considering the following questions.

   (a) From the data in the table alone, what would you expect to find about relative pollution levels in the five lakes?

   (b) In which lake might pollution problems be most long-lasting?

   (c) How confident are you about your inferences for parts (a) and (b)? What additional data would increase your confidence?

7. (a) Based on these data, how do you think American and Canadian viewpoints on industrial development might differ?

   (b) The occupations, ages, situations, and beliefs of the people living around the Great Lakes differ as widely as those of people anywhere in the world. List at least 20 different viewpoints about "maintaining the health of the Great Lakes" that might be held by people living in the Great Lakes area.

8. Consider with your group the following questions with reference to either of the two articles that follow: "Big Mackerel Attack" about the mackerel in British Columbia, or "Fishermen Fear They'll Be the Fall Guys" about the ocean fishery off Newfoundland.

   (a) What is the viewpoint of the person who wrote the article? What other viewpoints are expressed in the article?

   (b) Who do you think conducts research about the fish population? Who bears the cost of this?

   (c) Why do you think the research is done? Discuss the value of the research to people who depend on the fishery for their livelihood. Think in terms of one year, five years, and twenty years.

   (d) Besides people who make their living from fishing, who else do you think should have input into making the regulations?

   (e) What other information would you like to have, before forming an opinion about how much fishing should be allowed?

Big Mackerel Attack

For the first time in living memory, there will be no commercial fishing for Fraser River sockeye this year unless the runs turn out better than forecast. Wayne Saito, salmon coordinator for the Department of Fisheries and Oceans, says July, September and October returns are expected to be "poor." Any chance of the fishery opening will come in August, leaving British Columbia seiners and gillnetters high and dry for most, if not all, of the Fraser sockeye season. The closure deals a harsh blow to the salmon fleet, which normally makes 60 to 70 percent of its earnings from Fraser River salmon, and at least 50 percent of that from the premium-priced sockeye.

Sockeye runs have distinct high and low cycles that occur every four years, two of the most drastic downturns having occurred in the 1920s and 1960s. As recently as 1993, Fraser sockeye numbered 24 million, the best run since 1913. In a low year, the norm is three million to six million. But only 1.5 to 1.6 million are expected to return in 1996, the worst in 30 years.

Why such a low run? And does it preface a long-term crisis in salmon stocks? This year's returning sockeye were spawned in 1992 and went to sea during an extended El Niño, a pronounced warming of the Pacific Ocean currents off the coast of South America. This brought unusually warm water north to coastal British Columbia, along with millions of voracious mackerel which devoured huge numbers of juvenile salmon off Vancouver Island. During this so-called "big mac attack," one mackerel was found to have 14 young salmon in its stomach. The result: fewer juveniles than normal survived, reducing the 1996 sockeye run.

Other factors may also contribute to a low return.

Commercial fishing interests say native poaching on the Fraser in 1992 netted hundreds of thousands of fish that should have been allowed to spawn. Another problem, say environmentalists, is that smaller stocks can be inadvertently wiped out when they are mixed with larger stocks that are heavily fished.

DFO officials concede that habitat loss and pollution have put some stocks in jeopardy, particularly chinook and coho. But they deny there is an impending salmon collapse akin to the crash of the Atlantic cod stocks. With ocean temperatures returning to normal and the mackerel gone, there is hope that the sockeye will rebound. In the meantime, DFO has ordered the curb on sockeye fishing so enough fish will spawn to sustain future runs.

—Tom Koppel

Fishermen fear they'll be the fall guys

By GLEN WHIFFEN
The Evening Telegram

Many Newfoundland fishermen feel that despite positive signs, Ottawa is holding off on reopening closed fisheries until there is more pressure from fishermen to do so.

Roger Tucker of Foxtrap says he believes the federal government is taking this approach so they won't have to bear the blame should fishery fail again.

"The way I got it sized up, no matter if there are thousands of fish, they are waiting for the amount of pressure to build so that their hand is going to have to be forced from them to make a decision," he said.

"So if something happens that the fish declines again, or it migrates somewhere, they're going to be able to come back and say we didn't really feel like it was right to open it. They will say the only reason it was opened was because of pressure from fishermen and plant workers, and then they will be able to point the finger at us fellows."

Fishermen around Newfoundland have been reporting strong signs of cod through sentinel fishery surveys, high cod by-catch in other fisheries and recordings of large schools of fish on depth sounders.

There have also been reports of young cod around wharves, and in other areas where they haven't been seen in years. Offshore fishermen also report seeing a lot of cod while they are steaming to fishing grounds or while fishing other species.

Fishermen along the south coast of the province in fishing zone 3Ps have been arguing that the stocks there can support a commercial fishery in 1997, with a quota of a least 20,000 tonnes for the inshore.

Earl Johnson of North Harbour, Placentia Bay, said the federal Fisheries Department should listen to what the fishermen have to say about the stocks, but not just so they can shift any future blame.

"If anything goes wrong then they'd like to be able to say that we wanted the fishery open and that it's our fault, said Johnson. "I'd be willing to take a chance on it, but if they are going to give us a say, give us enough say to conserve the stocks."

Johnson said that the inshore fishermen should be the only ones taking part in a commercial fishery if it opens in 1997.

"If draggers come back on the scene the way they were before," he said, "we are going to be in trouble again fairly quick."

Tucker said Ottawa can forget scientific data and research if they are not willing to open their eyes to the physical evidence that's out there on the fishing grounds, being seen by fishermen.

"You can surmise and guess and listen to rumors to what's there, but when the physical evidence is there, that there are fish in an area, how can you dispute it?" he said.

"I don't know how long [federal fisheries] are going to wait before they are confident the stocks are strong enough to reopen a fishery. Right now they are afraid to open their mouth to say what's there because it seems like they are not really sure."

RISK/BENEFIT ANALYSIS

A risk/benefit analysis is a step-by-step process for making a decision or choosing a course of action. Research is an ongoing part of the process, valuable at every stage of the process.

- ▦ Define the issue to be considered.
- ▦ Assess the risks and benefits in the present situation, from as many viewpoints as possible.
- ▦ Identify several possible courses of action.
- ▦ Assess the risks and benefits of the different courses of action.
- ▦ Choose the "best" course of action.

The strategies for working with a group that are described in Chapter 2 can be useful throughout the risk/benefit analysis; use them to ensure that everyone has an opportunity to contribute to the discussion.

STS Exercise

Here are three situations for which your group can prepare a risk/benefit analysis, using the five steps outlined above. As you discuss the scenarios, be conscious of the scientific, technological, and societal aspects of the situation.

1. *A baby boy is born and is diagnosed as having Down Syndrome. An examination of the chromosome complement of his cells reveals that he does, in fact, have trisomy 21 – an extra 21st chromosome in each cell. This is characteristic of someone with the Down Syndrome. Doctors also detected the fact that the new-born had an obstruction of the digestive tract, but this could be corrected surgically with little risk involved. The parents, however, refused to permit the surgeons to operate. They argued that it would be better to allow the infant to die rather than let him grow up with a limited quality of life. They also felt that it would be hard on the other two children in the family. Since the doctors lacked the permission to operate, the infant died several days later.*

(a) Select two possible courses of action that could have been followed. For each, compare the risks and the benefits, being aware of who bears the risks and who reaps the benefits.

(b) Besides those of the parents and doctors, what other viewpoints might be considered? Should the power to decide lie solely with the parents, solely with the doctors, or with both? Or should any of the other viewpoints be given some weight in the question?

2. *The attractive weed known as purple loosestrife is rapidly displacing other plants in wetland areas of a number of states and provinces. Scientists have discovered a beetle, not native to North America, which eats and destroys loosestrife. These beetles have been introduced to areas where loosestrife grows.*

(a) What might be the harmful effects of purple loosestrife? How serious might these effects be in the environment?

(b) For the course of action that has been selected, what are some potential risks?

(c) Think of a different course of action, and describe the risks associated with it.

(d) Compare the potential benefits of the two courses of action.

3. *Many surveys have shown that a majority of couples would like their first child to be a boy. As well, numerous studies have shown that firstborns are more likely to be successful in life. If couples were able to select the sex of their firstborn, then the majority might be boys. Given that two-child families are more common in many societies, this might place female offspring at a disadvantage if they were more frequently the younger sibling of a male child. However, it could be argued that being able to predetermine the sex of an offspring would make every child a wanted child, including the female offspring.*

(a) What adverse effects might there be on society if the male/female ratio were altered so that there were many more males than females?

continued ▶

(b) How serious might these effects be?

(c) Suppose that it becomes general practice to choose the sex of children. Outline two or three different courses of action that could prevent the skewing of the male/female ratio. Discuss the risks and benefits of each, including risks to whom and benefits to whom. Which course of action would you recommend?

4. Select one of questions 1, 2, and 3. For this question, list facts that you would want to find if you were researching the issue. What else would be important to know, besides facts?

5. This question is based on the article that follows, "Saskatchewan Dam Wars Prove Nature Always loses."

(a) What is the viewpoint of the writer?

(b) Discuss the risks and benefits that are mentioned in the article.

(c) What similarities can you find between this issue and the one described in "Danube Diverted for Hydro Project" in Chapter 1? Are these similarities helpful for assessing the Saskatchewan situation?

6. This question is based on the other article that follow, "Gypsy Moth Outbreak May Lead to Quarantine."

(a) Carry out a risk/benefit analysis based only on what you read in the article.

(b) What further information would you like to have if you were doing an in-depth analysis of this issue?

7. It's common to find experts with background and training in the same field who express different opinions about an issue in their area of expertise.

(a) List two examples that illustrate this situation.

(b) If you were faced with a situation in which two experts in the same field disagreed about an issue, what factors would you consider before choosing to accept one view over the other?

(c) Suggest at least three other alternatives to accepting one view over the other.

Saskatchewan dam wars prove nature always loses

Short-term jobs, flood control take priority over wildlife

by David Suzuki

In battles for areas like the Stein Valley in B.C., Temagami in Ontario, James Bay in Quebec or the Amazon in Brazil, non-resident environmentalists are often accused of being "outsiders" who have no right sticking their noses in other people's business.

But the atmosphere, water, soil and biodiversity on the planet make up a single continuous complex of which we are all a part. The issues at stake matter to all of us. Take the Rafferty and Alameda dams in Saskatchewan.

The Moose Mountain Creek flows into the Souris River in Saskatchewan, crosses the border into North Dakota, curls back up into Manitoba, and empties into the Assiniboine River. The Souris River and Moose Mountain Creek flow through Prairie valleys supporting several rare and endangered plants that are part of a kind of ecosystem rapidly disappearing in Canada. In the U.S., the Souris supports a $4-million fishery and flows through two wildlife refuges that support some 22,000 ducks.

From time to time, the Souris overflows and in 1976, the town of Minot, N.D., was flooded for more than a month. The townspeople urged construction of the Burlington Dam for flood control but were opposed by the rural people who successfully stopped it.

In the mid-'80s the Saskatchewan government of Grant Devine proposed to build a coal-fired power station called Shand. It was to be air-cooled. North Dakota offered $41 million (US) if Saskatchewan would build a dam.

The American offer made the Rafferty Dam on the Souris feasible–it could control flooding downstream and the stored water could be used to cool Shand. However, international agreements require that at least half of the original water flow be guaranteed downstream to the U.S. In order to ensure a supply to fulfill that need, the

Continued on page 42

Saskatchewan dam wars prove nature always loses

Continued from page 41

Alameda dam on Moose Mountain Creek was started. So the U.S. offer made Rafferty possible and that, in turn, made Alameda necessary.

The dams will flood about 15 000 acres of land. But those acres are not just on flat plain, they are part of a ribbon of habitat for the endangered plants and a corridor in which wildlife can live and move.

Dam construction was started in June 1986 and then put on hold for the winter. In April 1989 the court ruled that the dam permits were illegal because a proper environmental impact assessment had not been made. In response, the federal government commissioned an environmental report. The report noted that the dams would have "significant impacts" on the environment and that there remained "significant information deficiencies."

In June, public meetings were held to allow people to comment on the report. Proponents of the dams stressed the benefits of jobs, flood control and agricultural water whereas opponents pressed for Phase 2 of the assessment–a full panel review with public hearings. Over the summer, Eric Bernston, the deputy premier of Saskatchewan, threatened that if dam construction did not begin by fall, the dams would never be built.

The benefits of the dams disappear on inspection. Downstream, the $4-million fishery and the ducks in North Dakota will all be put at risk while the quality of water reaching Manitoba has yet to be assessed.

Computer simulations show that even after the 1976 flood, Rafferty would only be 83-percent full if all water was retained for a year. Based on average rainfall, a dam built in 1912 would not have filled until 1952. Even without global warming, 75 percent of the annual flow in the Rafferty will evaporate during the summer.

The current projected costs of the dams and Shand are $1.3 billion and large projects like this are notorious for cost overruns.

Nevertheless, on Aug. 31, the environment minister issued a permit for construction of the dams. His decision must have been dictated by priorities of short-term jobs and flood control.

It would be far cheaper and simpler to encourage people to move away from chronic flood areas but human imperatives always seem to demand that nature conform to us rather than the other way around.

Suzuki is a writer, TV and radio host and a world-renowned geneticist. He is also a leading spokesman on social and environmental issues.

Gypsy moth outbreak may lead to quarantine

BY BRIAN RAU
TRURO BUREAU

An outbreak of the leaf-devouring gypsy moth has Agriculture Canada reconsidering regulations to restrict the movement of wood within the province.

A plant protection officer confirmed Thursday the department has asked the province's forest industry to agree to a zone (boundary line), which would require wood from the western part of Nova Scotia to be inspected before it crosses over to mills in the central and eastern regions of the province.

Gregg Cunningham said pressure from the U.S. to satisfy international quarantines, and domestic restrictions on the movement of potentially infested wood necessitates one of the three proposed boundary lines.

So far, the preferred line appears to be one that follows Highway 354 from Middle Sackville to Noel.

While populations of the gypsy moth are not nearly as high in Nova Scotia as they are in New England and other parts of the U.S., there are quarantined areas in the Annapolis Valley and in Kejimkujik National Park.

The moth is most dangerous in its caterpillar stage, during June and July, when it can eat up to a square metre of foliage by the time it matures.

"The gypsy moth is primarily a hardwood pest, but it's an opportunistic traveller and the female adult can lay eggs on softwoods, so the risk is always there," Mr. Cunningham said.

But sawmill operators from central and eastern Nova Scotia who purchase wood from suppliers in western Nova Scotia aren't convinced of the seriousness of the risk and oppose Agriculture Canada's proposal.

"It's going to cost us $80 a truckload to have the wood inspected," said Laurie Ledwidge, president of Ledwidge Lumber Co. in Enfield.

Continued on page 44

Gypsy moth outbreak may lead to quarantine

Continued from page 44

About 65 per cent of the mill's production comes from areas that will have to be inspected or possibly certified under the proposal.

The bottom line is consumers might have to pay more for lumber, which has already jumped in price by almost 20 per cent over the past two years.

"We'll have to try to get more for our lumber, to absorb the costs of the inspections", Mr. Ledwidge said.

Alan Rees, mill manager at Mactara Ltd., the province's biggest sawmill, said the proposal would have a severe impact on the Upper Musquodoboit mill's wood supply.

"Where they're proposing to draw the line would separate us from the major portion of our suppliers, and we can't live with that", he said.

Mr. Rees questioned the reasoning behind the proposal, and wondered if it might have something to do with concerns over the moth expressed by the Christmas tree industry.

"It appears what Agriculture Canada is doing is protecting the Christmas tree growers. It seems to me they're reacting to one part of the economy and not the other," he said.

A spokesman for the Nova Scotia Christmas Tree Council could not be reached for comment Thursday.

A draft of the proposal contains plant protection requirements governing the movement within Canada and from Canada and the U.S. for nursery stock, Christmas trees, forestry products with bark, and outdoor household articles that can harbor any life stage of the gypsy moth.

Mr. Cunningham said a sub-committee of the Nova Scotia Forest Products Association is expected to decide by Sept. 24 which option of the proposal they prefer.

He said restrictions on potentially infested wood going to the U.S. from western Nova Scotia could take effect by the end of October (when Christmas trees are traditionally exported) while restrictions on domestic movement could go into effect by April 3, 1997.

A forest technician in charge of monitoring the gypsy moth for the Nova Scotia Department of Natural Resources said populations of gypsy moth are low in the province.

Marty McCarthy said the insects usually only feed on hardwood species, such as oak trees, but he cautioned lumbermen should still be concerned because the moth can move outside quarantined areas into non-regulated zones. They gypsy moth was first detected in Nova Scotia in 1981.

PRESENTATIONS 4

"We are going to have to find ways of organizing ourselves co-operatively, sanely, scientifically, harmonically and in regenerative spontaneity with the rest of humanity around earth..."

R. Buckminster Fuller,
Operating Manual for Spaceship Earth

No single person in our society has the power to make decisions about issues in a social vacuum. Leaders, whether politicians, business tycoons, or community representatives, have to work with others members of society. Skills such as analyzing arguments, holding discussions, weighing risks and benefits, persuading others, developing compromise and consensus–all these are part of living in society. And, as you might expect, these skills improve with practice.

This chapter invites you to plan and make a presentation to an audience. By now you have had practice in identifying issues, generating ideas, and assessing viewpoints and opinions, and you are aware of the complexity of STS issues. By engaging in a debate, a role play, or a dramatic presentation, each participant, whether chairperson, researcher, debater, actor, or audience member, will draw upon the ideas and techniques you have been exploring in this book.

DEBATES

The debate is a traditional form of formal argument that is very much like a sport or a judicial trial. It has rules, time limits, and two teams who become winners and losers. A debate does not lead to consensus; it may, in fact, lead to greater polarization of opinion. But emotional appeals, heated arguments, and the thrust and parry of points and rebuttals can produce a thought-provoking and entertaining event. As a debater, you get great practice in marshaling arguments, public speaking, thinking under pressure, and convincing others of your viewpoint. This kind of experience can be valuable not only for a life in politics, but also for business and community affairs. The audience members, who ultimately vote to decide the winning team, are not passive viewers. They need all their skills of analytical thinking to assess the arguments of the two sides.

For a debate, as for an academic controversy, you need a statement that allows for two (and only two) sides to the issue. This is called the *resolution*, and is stated in the following way: "Be it resolved that ... (some action should be taken)." The team that argues for the resolution is called the Affirmative (A) team. The Negative (N) team argues against the resolution.

Depending on the size of your group, each team may consist of two or three people, so you need four to six debaters. You will also need a chairperson and a timekeeper, who may or may not be member of your group.

Once everyone agrees on the resolution, debaters will need to take some time to develop their arguments and prepare their speeches. For a serious debate, research that produces authentic facts and figures is essential preparation, and it might help your case if you can tell where and how you obtained them. A sense of humor can be a great asset. Jokes, amusing anecdotes, appeals to emotion, extrapolation of your opponents' ideas to ridiculous ends–all of these can help persuade the audience to favor your side.

The following list shows the sequence of events in a debate. The length of the speeches is agreed in advance and strictly enforced by the timekeeper. For a practice debate, such as the ones suggested in the Exercise below, speeches could be one minute each. If the speakers have done a lot of research, then two minutes each might be better, although the summing up speeches could still be one minute. The speakers are arranged on the platform as shown on page 48.

Chairperson

States the resolution and introduces the speakers.

Explains the rules and order of speakers.

Speaker A1

Clarifies the resolution, defining terms.

Argues in support of the resolution, supplying convincing evidence.

Introduces a plan showing how the resolution could be implemented.

(This is the only speech entirely prepared before the debate.)

Speaker N1

Challenges definitions, arguments, and evidence of Speaker A1.

Argues against the resolution, making new points.

Sums up why A1 was wrong or misguided, why the negative is correct.

Speaker A2

Counters arguments of N1.

Reiterates the good points of A1, modifying and adding as necessary in response to N1's arguments.

Attempts to anticipate points of N2.

Clarifies the affirmative position.

Speaker N2

Makes any new points.

Counters specific points of affirmative position.

Clarifies the negative position.

Chairperson

Announces a break for discussion (strictly timed, usually 2 to 3 minutes).

Speaker N3 (or N1 again)

Points out where the affirmative team failed to prove its points.

Sums up the negative position (no new points may be presented).

Speaker A3 (or A1 again)

Points out where the negative team failed to prove its points;

Makes a final review of the affirmative position (no new points may be presented).

Chairperson

Asks debaters to leave the room, and conducts a vote (by ballot or show of hands).

Invites debaters back and announces the winning team.

TO KEEP YOUR AUDIENCE FOCUSED ON THE RESOLU-
TION, YOU MIGHT WANT TO HAVE IT IN WRITING
WHERE EVERYONE CAN SEE IT.

KEEP TO THE ISSUE!

There is a great temptation during debates to resort to ad hominem arguments–
arguments focusing on the speaker rather than on the ideas presented. Resist this
temptation! The chairperson of a debate, like the Speaker in the House of Commons,
will interrupt if the speeches become rude or off the point. A debate is a spirited
discussion of cleverly expressed ideas, not a clash of personalities.

STS EXERCISE

1. There are many ways to write a resolution for a debate based on the article "Genetic Testing Boom Raises Ethical Questions" on the following page. In your group select which of the following you think would provide the fairest basis for a debate. (Both sides must be plausible.)

   (a) Be it resolved that all genetic testing of humans should be banned.

   (b) Be it resolved that employers should never have access to the results of genetic testing of their employees.

   (c) Be it resolved that genetic testing for conditions for which there is no cure should be banned.

   (d) Be it resolved that genetic testing should only be allowed in publicly funded and publicly controlled hospitals and universities.

2. From the articles reprinted in earlier chapters, select two and write a resolution for each that could be used as the basis for a debate. (There may be several different aspects that could be the basis for a debate, so you need to identify a central issue.) In your group, discuss everyone's resolutions to determine whether they have caught the essence of the issue, and are stated in a form that could be used for a debate.

3. Arrange for a live audience, and run a debate on one of the resolutions from questions 1 or 2. (For practice beforehand in thinking and speaking on your feet, you might want to make up a more frivolous resolution and use it as an introduction to the enjoyments of the debating game.)

Genetic testing boom raises ethical questions

BY MARIANNE KULKA

Genetic testing is booming beyond our ability to control it, warns an expert on ethics in genetics.

Even though scientists can detect genes that are linked to specific disorders and conditions, they may not be able to do anything about it, says Neil Holtzman.

"We discover the means of detecting before we discover the means to treat," said Holtzman, professor of Pediatrics at Johns Hopkins Hospital in Baltimore and chairman of the Task Force on Genetic Testing in the U.S.

Genetic tests are only beneficial if society sets some guidelines, he said during the recent Dr. Bea Flowlow memorial lecture at the University of Calgary.

"No testing should be done without the consent of the people being tested. They need to be told that other people may gain access to their test results."

Holtzman said it's possible to set up a bank of tissue specimens to genetically track criminals—much the same way as fingerprints are used today.

But this opens up ethical problems because researchers can use these specimens for question-able testing–anything from aggressive behaviour to obscure genetic diseases to intelligence.

Holtzman said there are also problems because genetic tests are not always accurate. "In any single individual the predictive value of the test may not be so great."

For example, "we don't know whether or not genetic testing will increase the lifespan of people with the breast cancer gene."

Genetic testing can tell a couple their risk for having a child with a genetic disorder but it does not eliminate that risk, he said.

"The press has a

responsibility not to oversell the benefits of genetic testing," he added.

In the U.S., a lot of genetic tests are done by privately-funded clinics. In Canada, genetic testing is mostly done by publicly-funded hospitals and universities. "In Canada, there is more regionalization and more co-ordination."

In both countries, there is an expanding commercial interest in genetic testing, he says. "There is money to be made by offering these tests."

"Increases in the number of medical geneticists and genetic counsellors are not keeping pace with these pressures and are not likely to," Holtzman said.

As genetic technology becomes more complex, he said that genetic specialists have important roles as counsellors, teachers, researchers and standard-setters.

They must protect the public from inappropriate services and ensure affordable access to necessary services as consumer demand increases. There are many clinics doing very complicated procedures and it is often difficult to monitor each one, said Holtzman. "There are serious questions of quality."

Another ethical dilemma is that the majority of genetic diseases still can't be cured even if the underlying genes are found.

Research to find the cures for genetic diseases will not increase even though more genetic tests will be available, Holtzman believes.

There are also "serious questions" on whether we have sufficient knowledge to offer these tests."

"People want certainty if they are going to make very drastic decisions and that is understandable," he says. "Very often, people are not told about uncertainty."

ROLE PLAYING

As a presentation to an audience, a role play is fundamentally different from a debate. In a debate, an issue is reduced to a single statement and the debating teams present arguments in an attempt to persuade people one way or the other. The teams may do in-depth research and present complex ideas, but there are essentially two ways of thinking: affirmative and negative. In a role play, there may be as many ways of thinking as there are participants. Rather than reducing real life to a single question, a role play simulates real life with all its complexities and contradictions.

Business plans and public policy-making must often move forward even when there is no general consensus on what should be done about an issue. There will always be disagreement about such questions as the use of nuclear reactions or fossil fuels as power sources, disposal of garbage, preventing the spread of communicable diseases, using pesticides, and dozens of others. In real life there are few simple questions with yes-or-no, all-or-nothing answers. Compromise and conciliation are essential. In order to come to a decision about the best possible course of action, a public body may invite input from as many people and groups as possible at a public forum. All participants have an opportunity to present their own perspective, backed up by their own experiences and their own research. A simulation of a public hearing, with group members playing the roles of a variety of people, is a dramatic way to present an issue to an audience.

COMMISSIONS AND TASK FORCES

Governments at all levels–from municipal to federal–set up commissions or task forces from time to time to investigate issues. Often they will hold a series of "hearings" where any interested individuals or groups can make a presentation outlining their concerns. After hearing all the presentations and doing their own research, the commission or task force prepares a report summarizing their findings and recommending a course of action. In their recommendations they need to be realistic, recognizing that factors such as budget limitations and the public's preconceptions may limit what can be done. The recommendations made by commissions and task forces are rarely implemented in full; sometimes they may be ignored completely. Even so, the hearings can still be beneficial because they allow the airing of a variety of different views about the issue. The public and politicians are informed simply by following the progress of the hearing, as reported in the media.

STS Exercise

1. To see how effective a role play can be, do one about your own community. The next page has suggestions for holding a simulated hearing to

   (a) determine whether your public water supply is safe for drinking, and

   (b) make recommendations about future courses of action. (If there is an issue currently in the news, you might want to use it instead and adapt the guidelines. Or you could use the partially scripted role play about acid rain that is included in the appendix on page 61.) At the end of the hearing the chairperson should be able to deliver an opinion on the first question and describe the risks and benefits of two or three possible scenarios.

2. Hold a "debriefing session" about the role play, considering the following questions.

   (a) What research would have given more credibility to the various roles?

   (b) What kinds of scientific knowledge were needed at the hearing?

   (c) Whose viewpoints were more short-term, and whose were more long-term?

   (d) What, if any, group strategies were used at any stage in the role play? What ones could have been used?

   (e) When did risk/benefit analysis enter into the discussion? (If it didn't, when should it have?)

SUGGESTIONS FOR ROLE PLAYING A HEARING ABOUT PUBLIC WATER SUPPLIES

For this role play, you will need a small amount of research. You could re-read the article "Public or Private–Who Should Control Municipal Water Supplies?" on page 27 and investigate the following questions about your community:

- What is the source of the water (river, lake, well)?
- Where is the water intake?
- How is the water treated (what is added, etc.)?
- In your immediate area, where are landfills, industries, farms, sewage treatment plants, etc.?
- What goes on upstream and/or downstream?
- Is there any history of water-borne parasites in your community or any nearby communities?
- How often is the water tested, and what is it tested for?

You will need to work with at least eight people. The task force itself could be a single person who also chairs the hearing, or there could be three people on the task force, with one acting as chairperson. Everyone else will represent different individuals, each with their own viewpoint. (If you have many people, two or three could work together to develop the role of one individual.) Different individuals could have concerns about:

- chlorine-containing compounds
- effect on the level of taxation of improving the quality
- susceptibility to infection of people with weak immune systems
- presence of heavy metals such as lead and mercury
- cloudiness of the water
- odor of the water
- need for additional sources of water

You could select roles similar to these, ensuring that you have a good representation of the people who make up your community.

- salesperson, 30, mother of two-year-old, expecting another child
- retired construction worker, 75,
- doctor, 40, specializing in AIDS patients
- child, 10, keen swimmer
- manager, 50, employed by fertilizer factory
- owner, 45, of company making water treatment supplies
- tourist guide, 25
- town council member, 60
- worker, 30, at pulp and paper factory
- fisherman, 40
- advocate of alternative medicine, 20

For the hearing itself, set time limits for each person's presentation, then allow questions by all representatives and audience.

DRAMATIC PRESENTATIONS

The arts–music, painting, sculpture, dance, literature, theater, movies–reflect a society and its values. Songs, stories, and movies can illustrate ideas, grip an audience's attention, and leave people thinking long after the performance is finished.

For any group presentation, consider using all the talents of your team. You could write verses to a song with alternating voices for and against a specific issue, produce a play complete with sets and costumes, choreograph a dance illustrating some effect of technology on society, or videotape some real-life vignettes. Use group techniques and analytical thinking skills in the preparation, and let your imaginations roam. The issue may be serious, your analysis may be well-researched and thought out, but your creative presentation can put some spice into your ideas.

THE FICTION IN SCIENCE FICTION

Science fiction and its relatives, fantasy and supernatural fiction, provide especially fertile ground for exploring issues related to science, technology, and society. To distinguish what is remotely possible from what is pie-in-the-sky, a solid background in science is helpful. But yesterday's pie-in-the-sky may become today's reality. For example, *Ender's Game*, by Orson Scott Card (1977), was published many years before the Internet was anything but imagination, yet in this story the "Net," complete with communication and simulation games, is central to the action. *2010: Odyssey Two*, by Arthur C. Clarke (1968) tells of life on Jupiter's moon Europa; in 1996 there was serious speculation by scientists about this very possibility.

Classic visionary tales such as Aldous Huxley's *Brave New World* (1932) and George Orwell's *Nineteen Eighty-four* (1948), depict a future–our present–in which technology has come to take a predominant place in society. Both are eerily prescient of developments that are at the heart of many issues of today.

Movies such as *2001: A Space Odyssey* (1968), *Poltergeist* (1982), *Blade Runner* (1982) or *Jurassic Park* (1993), in addition to being suspenseful thrillers, are powerful fables of science and technology run amok, and invite reflection on the role of scientists and technologists, and the connections among science, technology, and society.

STS Exercise

1. Read the article "Caffeine Addiction Not a Myth" (page 58). Allow yourselves a limited time, about 10 minutes, to identify the scientific questions and consider various viewpoints, then make up a short skit to illustrate the ideas in the article.

2. (a) Of the movies that people in your group have seen in the past two years, which ones were based on STS issues, either explicitly or implicitly?

   (b) Identify the issues raised and identify the viewpoints presented.

   (c) How "grounded" in fact was the scientific and technological information that these movies used? How much does that matter in the short run (while you watch the film) and in the long run (as you ruminate over the ideas later)?

3. In an anthology of science fiction stories, select one that presents, or is based on, an STS issue. Read it and discuss the ideas with your group.

4. In a book or on the Internet, find an example of a painting that clearly deals with an STS issue. Bring a copy for the group, and hold a discussion based on the following questions.

   (a) What is the issue, and how are the aspects of science and technology dealt with?

   (b) What is the artist's viewpoint?

   (c) In your opinion, what (if any) role should artists play in focusing public attention on issues?

5. Discuss the advantages and disadvantages of debates, role plays, and dramatic presentations as a means of presenting an issue to a group. For each, think of at least one situation where it would be suitable and one where it would not be.

Caffeine addiction not a myth

Chicago (AP)–They're not called java junkies for nothing.

Medical research now confirms what coffee drinkers long have suspected: Some people get so hooked on caffeine that they have many of the same dependency traits of alcoholics or drug addicts.

But caffeine-aholics can rest easy–if their jittery, jangly nerves will let them.

"In general, caffeine use has not been asso-ciated with serious health risks," said lead researcher Roland Griffiths, a professor of psychiatry and neuroscience at Johns Hopkins University School of Medicine in Baltimore.

"Our findings in and of themselves should not be used as a reason to quit caffeine use."

In a recent survey, members of a focus group were asked to express their opinion about "the most important issue facing society today." They were given three lines and one minute to respond. One respondent paused briefly and then wrote, "Issues are too complex to be limited to three lines and one minute."

Perhaps because revolutionary advances in science and technology are occurring so rapidly, individuals are often expected to move equally quickly. But in a myriad of ways, the forms and changes of "society" are more difficult to comprehend, and more difficult to influence, than those of "science" or "technology." Some of our most fundamental issues arise where the three overlap. Perhaps because of the breakneck speed of developments, these issues are frequently distilled and reduced to "sound bites"–brief, snappy, often inflammatory, and too-often oversimplified.

It is the hope of the authors that, when you are confronted with the opportunity to express an opinion or influence a course of action, you will be able to apply the ideas and techniques in this book:

- identifying aspects of science and technology that underlie many societal issues;

- recognizing the value of everyone having at least a rudimentary understanding of fundamental concepts of science and technology;

- eliciting opinions from others in a constructive manner;

- appreciating the viewpoints of others, even when you disagree with their opinions;

• finding, interpreting, and assessing data and information from many sources in order to develop an informed opinion;

• reflecting on your own opinions and how you form them;

• accepting that exploring and resolving issues are the responsibility of everyone in a free and open society.

"...We are not going to be able to operate our spaceship Earth successfully nor for much longer unless we see it as a whole spaceship and our fate as common. It has to be everybody or nobody."

(R. Buckminster Fuller)

APPENDIX: ALTERNATIVE ROLE PLAY– THE ACID RAIN DEBATE[1]

How can you explore an issue as many-sided and controversial as acid rain? When even scientists and government officials are hard-pressed to keep up with research findings about the environmental impact, industrial connections, and social and ecological implications of acid rain, how can anyone expect to understand the issues? Once you have read enough to have an overview of the problem of acid rain in North America, you can sort out your own opinions about acid rain, its sources, and its consequences with this simulation. So familiarize yourself with the cast of characters, brush up on your acid rain facts, and prepare to make some heavy decisions about an issue that strikes at the heart of STS questions. By the time you have completed the simulation, you should be able to describe the causes and effects of acid rain to anyone who wants to know and to suggest several concrete solutions to this problem.

SETTING THE SCENE

The activity is designed for about 24 people: 4 members of the International Commission on Acid Rain and 20 characters who make presentations. If you have fewer people, you can omit a few of the characters; if you have more, expand the size of the commission. The commission, a joint effort by Canada and the United States, is going to conduct a public hearing. On the basis of the testimony it hears, the commission will make recommendations to both governments on specific ways to solve the acid rain problem.

---

[1]Adapted with permission from: Roger Bybee, Mark Hibbs, and Eric Johnson, "The Acid Rain Debate", in *The Science Teacher,* April 1984.

The members of the commission should select a chairperson and a secretary from among themselves. The chairperson will be responsible for recognizing speakers, maintaining order, and speaking for the commission. The secretary keeps a record of each person testifying (name, occupation, and group represented) and summarizes the views of each speaker. The characters should become familiar with their own roles and be prepared to speak about their point of view.

At the hearing, each witness is allowed to speak for 10 minutes. At the close of the hearing, the commission members meet in private to compile a list of their recommendations. In reaching a decision, the commission must be aware of the international ramifications of the acid rain problem. Commission members will need to record for their own use the points made in the presentations. At the close of the session, the chairperson will announce their recommendations.

After the hearing, reconvene to discuss the implications of the hearing and the commission's recommendations:

- Which testimonies might have been biased and in what way? Do you think all the testimonies were biased? Is bias a useful criterion for assessing testimonies?

- Can the commission make valuable and sound recommendations based on the testimonies it heard?

- On what criteria did the commission base its decisions?

- Was the commission fair to all interested parties? Should fairness be an issue?

- Did the commission weigh and then balance the risks and benefits that will arise from its decisions?

- Can the commission's recommendations realistically be implemented?

- Did the commission's recommendations address the international aspects of acid rain?

GUIDING THE COMMISSION

As members of the International Commission on Acid Rain, you are expected to be non-partisan. You are to make recommendations to the Canadian and U.S. governments about how they should individually or jointly deal with the problem of acid rain. You will make these recommendations after conducting a public hearing where private citizens, representatives of industry, and government officials share their information, opinions, and suggestions. As commission members, the following questions should guide your recommendations.

- Does Canada have any responsibilities to the United States? Does the United States have any responsibilities to Canada?
- Does private industry have a responsibility to citizens, to the government, and, in particular, to foreign governments? Do citizens and governments have responsibilities to private industry?
- If governments mandate pollution control by industry, do the governments have a responsibility to help pay for the necessary equipment, such as scrubbers?
- How can an industry's right to conduct business and create jobs be balanced with concerns about human and environmental health?
- Who is responsible for supporting research on acid rain? Is more research necessary? Can decisions be made in the absence of complete information?
- Does acid rain ever have any beneficial effects? If so, who benefits?
- Who should be responsible for the costs of reducing acid rain? Industry? Government? Citizens? And what, precisely, are those costs?

CHARACTER ROLES

1. *Hao Ling/Wen-Zhi Chen, age 28, geologist for the U.S. Geological Survey*

From experience, you understand that unbuffered soils are sensitive to acid rain and that soil acidification can have far-reaching consequences. One is the leaching of metals such as aluminum and iron, which can harm plants. Plant nutrients may be lost from susceptible soils. Some soils, such as those where Canada's forestry industry thrives, are naturally acidic but sensitive to increases in acidity. Thus, while additional research under field conditions is clearly necessary, studies already indicate that acid rain threatens both aquatic and terrestrial systems.

2. *Alex/Alexis Scott, age 37, chemist for Ontario Hydro, which provides electrical power for the Province of Ontario*

Ontario Hydro is the second largest source of SO_2 within the province and largest industrial source of NO_3 Ontario Hydro's coal-fired stations produce about 20 percent of the total emissions of these two pollutants in the province. Hydro is active in controlling SO_2 emissions by using only washed coal, which reduces sulfur levels by 15 to 20 percent. Hydro is also installing low NO_3 burners and SO_2 scrubbers to combat acid rain. You would urge the commission to require similar standards for SO_2 and NO_3 sources in the United States, since Hydro's actions alone are not effective because polluted air masses enter Canada from the United States.

3. *Julia/Jason Kirk, age 36, consulting meteorologist based in Toronto, Ontario*

As a member of a Canadian-U.S. research group, you have determined that the levels of transboundary pollution depend on prevailing wind and weather patterns. The net flow of sulfur is from south to north across the U.S.-Canadian border. On the average, three to four times as much sulfur crosses into Canada as moves into the United States, although the flow of sulfur from U.S. sources to Canadian air space is close to the total Canadian emissions in volume—5.5 million tonnes. You feel strongly that the commission should consider these data in making its recommendations.

4. *Hannah/Jacob Frisch, age 62, officer with the Minnesota Department of Natural Resources (DNR)*

Although DNR studies have not yet found an acidified Minnesota Lake, one quarter of Minnesota's 12 000 lakes have been identified as susceptible to acid rain. Canadian studies show that in addition to the threat to fish, amphibians, including salamanders and frogs, are drastically affected by acid rain. Because the salamander plays an essential role in the food chain, its disappearance would negatively affect waterfowl, such as loons, and mammals, such as skunks and shrews, that eat salamanders. Therefore, you believe the commission should consider that acid rain threatens wildlife as much as fish, amphibians, and aquatic plants.

5. *Leroy/Loretta Nelson, age 55, owner of Nelson's Lodge on the edge of Minnesota's Boundary Waters*

Your lodge caters to fishing enthusiasts drawn to the lakes of the Boundary Waters. While a report to the legislative commission on Minnesota resources found that no lake in the state was acidic or acidified, Minnesota Department of Natural Resources officers have told you that because of soil types and granite bedrock in your area, the local lakes are sensitive to acid deposition. Moreover, highly prized walleye pike, smallmouth bass, and lake trout comprise a major portion of the fish in these susceptible waters. If these lakes become acidic, fish populations will probably decline: this is turn would reduce the number of resorts and outfitter operations in the area by at least one half. You are representing these businesses. Acidification of Boundary Water lakes could cut down the volume of your industry from $63 million to $21 million annually; lost jobs are estimated to be 3000. You will urge the commission to take immediate steps toward eliminating acid rain.

6. *Lyle/Lucille Butler, age 51, farmer from Lakefield, Ontario*

You live in an area that is reportedly threatened by U.S.-produced acid rain. Although you've heard that acid rain can damage crops such as spinach, lettuce and beans, and can reduce yields of some crops such as beets, carrots, radishes, and broccoli, other crops have had higher yields thanks to the fertilizing effects of acid rain. In your case, corn yields have not declined, but occasionally have increased. You feel the commission should recognize that acid precipitation can sometimes be beneficial.

7. *Tanya/Carl Ryman, age 47, professor of architecture at MIT*

As a professor of architecture, you feel strongly that something should be done to curtail acid rain if for no other reason than to spare some of the great buildings of the world from slow destruction by acid rain. In Athens, marble sculptures dating from the fifth century BC are turning to soft gypsum. The cause is air pollution—in particular acid-producing pollutants. The Parthenon, the Taj Mahal, and the Colosseum, as well as U.S. landmarks, including the Statue of Liberty, the Lincoln Memorial, and the Washington Monument, are being harmed by acid washings. The President's Council on Environmental Quality estimated in 1979 that the annual cost of architectural damage in the United States was nearly $2 billion.

8. *Elliott/Brenda Jones, age 44, union representative of U.S. coal miners*

Legislation has been introduced in the U.S. Congress to mandate a 10 million ton annual reduction in SO_2, by 1990 in 31 eastern states. Coal industry officials have testified before a Senate committee that 98 600 mining jobs would be lost in the Appalachian and Midwest coal regions if this legislation becomes law. Although you cannot vouch for the accuracy of these figures, you would like the commission to be aware of the effects this type of legislation would have on regional economies. You will ask the commission to weigh the costs and benefits carefully. The wrong legislation could destroy the already depressed economies of these regions.

9. *Theresa/Paul Duchamps, age 33, environmental engineer for Provincial Mining Company, Manitoba, which produces nickel and manages several large mining and smelting operations*

Your company would like the commission to consider recommending action to return acidified lakes to their normal pH by liming rather than by strict and costly pollution control laws. In liming, a neutralizing agent, such as line or limestone, is added to a body of water. According to one estimate, liming 468 of the most acidic lakes in Adirondacks to a pH of 6 would cost about $4 million per year. The addition of scrubbers to 50 of the oldest coal burning power plants east of the Mississippi is estimated to cost between $7 billion and $14 billion for capital costs and between $1 billion and $3.6 billion for annual operating costs. The benefits of liming appear within 1 year; scrubbers take 3 to 5 years to build. In Provincial's opinion, liming is an attractive option that the commission should consider strongly.

10. *Marion/Gabriel Saracho-Mendez, age 29, representative of the U.S. Environmental Protection Agency (EPA)*

The current EPA position is that some proposed methods of halting acid rain might foster worse problems. In addition, the agency contends that much acid rain is caused locally, contrary to the theory that acid rain in the north-eastern United States and Canada is traceable to coal-powered plants in the Midwest. EPA believes acid rain requires additional scientific study before corrective measures are adopted. Some EPA researchers are studying how much acid rain is produced naturally.

11. *Edward/Lynne Genilo, age 54, president of Acme Steel Company, Pittsburgh*

Your region of the United States, in particular its steel industry, emits high levels of SO_2. Many local weather systems apparently carry SO_2 particulates into eastern Canada where they are deposited in acid rain. Your industry is attacked for contributing to the problem. Some experts are urging government agencies to require your plant to install pollution control equipment, such as scrubbers, to reduce the emissions. The equipment will cost $100 million to $250 million and, in addition, will demand more energy. Such a regulation could force your plant to close at a time when it is struggling to compete with imported steel from Japan. You will urge the commission to continue to investigate the problem but to refrain from making any recommendations for regulating pollution emissions until it is proven without a doubt that your plant is responsible for acid rain.

12. *Helen/Marc Poisson, age 27, Canadian forestry official*

Some researchers report that there is no proof that current levels of acid rain are significantly harming the terrestrial environment. In studies with simulated acid rain, the pH of the acid solutions used in the experiments that show adverse effects are usually lower than those normally occurring in rain. It is true that the leaching of nutrients from soil by acid rain could result in impoverished tree growth, but damage of this nature would take a long time to build up. Studies in Ontario do not yet show impaired tree growth. Although you are concerned about the problem of acid rain and you have no specific suggestions, you wanted to present recent research findings to the commission.

13. *Penelope/George Laplace, age 45, president of Canadian Paper Products, Inc.*

Most of the areas from which your company gets timber are located in regions where the pH of rain ranges from 4.2 to 4.5, as identified by the Ontario Ministry of the Environment. Rain of this acidity is reported to reduce tree growth and to kill many plant species, including some of the pines that are the mainstay of your industry. Because the forest industry is Canada's largest, worth more than $10 billion annually in eastern Canada alone, you want the commission to recommend immediate restrictions on sources of SO_2 and NO_3, such as certain industries and coal-fired power plants. If acid rain is not reduced to some extent, we can expect serious soil and forest effects in the next 25 to 100 years.

14. *Kim/Sanford Johnson, age 42, freelance writer working on an article on acid rain*

Although as a writer you try to remain objective, you have uncovered certain facts about acid rain that you think will interest the commission. The causes of acid rain include not only industrial pollution, but also automobile emissions, which account for much of the locally produced acid rain. Tall smokestacks built by utilities and industry reduce local pollution but transport acid droplets over great distances. Such information on dispersion should be useful in developing solutions to the problem.

15. *Alice/Neil Shiring, age 35, representative for General Motors of Windsor, Ontario*

The commission must consider all the facts before making decisions. Specifically, you will point out that in the United States, the President's Council on Environmental Quality stated that "insufficient knowledge exists about the explicit causes and total effects of acid rain...." Any new and unnecessary pollution control measures required of industries such as yours could have devastating effects on the industry and eventually the national economy. You would be forced to pass the costs for pollution control on to the consumer. You remind the commission that the costs of pollution control are not only direct but also indirect because your suppliers pass on their added costs to you. With the increase in Japanese and European automobile production, North American industries can remain competitive only by keeping production costs down. You will point out to the commission that any acid rain legislation affects all parts of society.

16. *Harold/Lisa Schmidt, age 32, public relations representative for Ohio River Valley Power Company*

In response to an increasing demand for energy, your company plans to build a new power plant, either a conventional coal-fired or a nuclear power plant. Your company is interested in the commission's recommendations because they may affect which type of plant you build. Even if the public is strongly opposed, Ohio River Valley Power will decide to build the more economical nuclear plant if costly restrictions are imposed on emissions from coal-fired plants. Although your company is somewhat impartial on acid rain, you want the commission to consider your situation and to make recommendations as soon as possible.

17. *Jeannette/François Durand, age 50, Deputy Minister of the Environment, Canada*

You plan to make the following statement on behalf of the Canadian Minister of the Environment:

"The solution to the acid rain problem is very straightforward. We must reduce drastically the amount of acid-causing pollution emitted in both countries. We already have the necessary technology: emission controls on smokestacks and cars and the ability to wash coal to cut down on the amount of sulfur released into the atmosphere. The argument against these solutions is cost, which admittedly is considerable; but the cost of not acting threatens forestry, tourism, and fishing. Building and automobile surfaces deteriorate each day. We may find that in the long run the cost to health has been great. No individual or group ever has the right to endanger the environmental health of a nation or a continent. Therefore, I urge you to recommend to both the Canadian and U.S. governments that immediate steps be taken to remedy the problem of acid rain."

18. *Malcolm/Barbara Gorden, age 53, Governor of Kentucky*

As a governor from the Ohio River Valley, you are well aware that acid rain is an international problem that should be addressed immediately. However, you will urge the commission to proceed thoughtfully and cautiously, examining all aspects of the problem before making recommendations. Your state is one of the leading producers in the United States. It has major sources of SO_2 and NO_3, particularly in the northern industrialized area that borders Ohio. Restrictions on industries and electrical utilities could have serious economic repercussions in your state.

19. *Marjorie/Michael Prince, age 30, Sierra Club lobbyist*

The commission, you believe, must take immediate action against SO_2-and NO_3–producing industries. After all, research has shown that these industries are responsible for acid rain. Waiting for 5 or 10 years of government investigation may cost the environment dearly. In response to advocates of such remedies as liming, you will point out that liming requires 9 kg per surface hectare per year, which means several tonnes even for small lakes. Although liming may return the pH to normal, metal concentrations will still remain at levels toxic to fish. Also the neutralizing effect wears off in 3 to 4 years. Liming may be a short-term remedy, but it is not a solution. Consider the logistics of dumping tonnes of lime into the thousands of lakes in Canada and portions of the United States!

20. *Walter/Wendy Freeman, age 37, professor of ecology at Carleton University, Ottawa, Ontario*

You would like to make the commission aware that acid rain threatens the environment and ultimately human health. Studies have shown a direct relationship between the severity of health problems and the level of air pollution as measured by the concentrations of suspended particulate matter, especially sulfates and SO_2 in industrial and urban settings. Acidification of water supplies could release metals from rocks, soils, or plumbing. In addition, the inhalation of sulfur particulates may cause chronic bronchitis and emphysema. Although none of these assertions has been proven, some evidence supports the validity of these hypotheses.

REFERENCES

A Sourcebook of Biotechnology Activities, Rasmussen, A., and Matheson, R., National Association of Biology Teachers, 11250 Roger Bacon Drive, #19, Reston, Virginia, USA, 22090, 1990.

Basic Genetics: A Human Approach, 2nd ed., BSCS, Kendall/Hunt Publishing Co., 1990. This is one of the very few genetics resources that deals with human genetics at the high school level. Includes a number of case studies.

Biotechnology Unzipped: A personal journey of discovery about biotechnology: facts, opinions, regulations, opportunities, and thoughts about the future. As balanced a book as is possible was this author's goal, and he has done it well.

Creative Role Playing Exercises in Science and Technology, Social Science Education Consortium, Inc., Boulder, Colorado, 1989. Three well-worked out role plays: AIDS, Nuclear Fuel, and Waste Disposal.

Population Reference Bureau, 2213 M Street, N.W., Washington, D.C., 20037. The source for any information pertaining to the world population issue. Particularly useful is the annual world population data sheet.

A Portfolio of Teaching Ideas for High School Biology, Honour Specialist Biology Teachers, FEUT, 1995, published by Trifolium Books Inc., 1996. A collection of 36 innovative biology activities for Grades 9-12.

Roman's Notes on DNA, Romaniuk, Roman, Trifolium Books Inc., 1997. A light, chatty writing style, and lots of ideas for how to remember difficult to recall concepts. As well, an introduction to some pros and cons of biotechnology, and a wonderfully extensive gloosary of terms.

Science and Social Issues, Newton, David, J. Weston Walch Pub., 1992; available from MIND Resources Ltd., Box 126, Kitchener, Ontario, N2 3W9.

Science and Society: Decision-making Episodes for Exploring Society, Science, and Technology. Stahl, Nancy, and Stahl, Robert, Addison-Wesley, 1995. A fine collection of decision-making episodes for exploring society, science, and technology.

Science and Technology in Society, The Association for Science Education, College Lane, Hatfield, Herts AL109AA, U.K. This series, often referred to as the SATIS program, is a collection of case studies, background information, and exercises dealing with a variety of science and technology issues. Must presently be ordered directly from the U.K.

Science, Technology, Society: Investigating and Evaluating STS Issues and Solutions. Hungerford, Harold et al., Stipes Publishing Co., 10-12 Chester St., Champaign, Illinois, 1990.

Science/Technology/Society: Activities and Resources for Secondary Science and Social Studies, Singleton, Laurel, ed.; order from SSEC, 3300 Mitchell Lane, Suite 240, Boulder; CO 80301-2296, phone (303) 492-8154, Cat. item #379-9; price US $23.95 plus $5 shipping and handling.

Simulations in Recombinant DNA, Edwards, Lois, Trifolium Books Inc., 1997. Excellent hands-on paper and pencil simulations of recombinant DNA processes. A great aid in understanding difficult-to-comprehend processes. Includes an issues-related exercise.

Social Issues, OSSTF Resource Booklets. Topics include nuclear issues, race relations, death education, and adolescent suicide.

Social Issues II, OSSTF Resource Booklets. Topics include AIDS, eating disorders, substance abuse, and violence.

The State of the World, 1995, Brown, Lester R. (Ed.), W.W. Norton Co., 1995. An overview of environmental issues taken from a global perspective. Like others in this series, this volume focuses on sustainable development.

STS: Investigating and Evaluating STS Issues and Solutions, Volk, Trudi et al, Stipes Publishing Co., 10 Chester Street, Champaign, IL (USA) 61820, ph.: 217-356-8391.

Wisdom of the Elders, Knudtson, Peter, and Suzuki, David, Stoddart Publishing Co., Toronto 1992. The ecological view of indigenous groups around the world.

CREDITS

The authors and publisher would like to thank the following for granting permission to reproduce in this book, the specific article indicated.

The Calgary Herald
   "Keeping Deer in Check: Population Boom Poses Dilemma," Bruce Masterman.

Associate Press
   "Danube Diverted for Hydro Project: Slovakia Goes Ahead Despite Hungarian Protest," in *The Calgary Herald,* November 11, 1992.

Equinox
   "Why Diamonds Are Not an Esker's Best Friend," Ed Struzik, April 1995.

Maclean's Magazine
   "Seeking Redress." Patricia Chisholm, September 9, 1996.

The Toronto Star Syndicate
   "Clean up Great Lakes, Watchdog Demands," Brian McAndrew, February 17, 1994.

Canadian Geographic Enterprises
   "Big Mackerel Attack," in *Canadian Geographic Magazine,* Tom Koppel, July/August 1996.

The Evening Telegram
   "Fishermen Fear They'll Be the Fall Guys," Glen Whiffen, September 14, 1996.

Southam
   "Saskatchewan Dam Wars Prove Nature Always Loses," in *The Calgary Herald,* David Suzuki, September 29, 1989.

The Chronicle Herald and The Mail-Star
   "Gypsy Moth Outbreak May Lead to Quarantine," September 13, 1996.

The Calgary Herald
   "Genetic Testing Boom Raises Ethical Questions," Marianne Kuka, 1995.

Associated Press
   "Caffeine Addiction Not a Myth," in *The Globe and Mail*, October 12, 1994.